Decolonial Daughter:
Letters from a Black Woman
to Her European Son

Decolonial Daughter:
Letters from a Black Woman
to Her European Son

Lesley-Ann Brown

Published by Repeater Books
An imprint of Watkins Media Ltd

19-21 Cecil Court
London
WC2N 4EZ
UK
www.repeaterbooks.com
A Repeater Books paperback original 2018
1

Distributed in the United States by Random House, Inc., New York.

Cover design: Johnny Bull
Typography and typesetting: Stuart Davies
Typefaces: Meridien

ISBN: 9781912248094
Ebook ISBN: 9781912248100

Printed and bound in the United Kingdom

Contents

for my

ancestors

Introduction

What have the Romans ever done for us?
— Monty Python, *Life of Brian*

What better gift could a mother give her child than the knowledge of who came before him or her, a narrative that her child could use to navigate this one?

I always knew that I wanted to write a book of letters to my son — to share some of my reflections and experiences in life in the hopes that it would better equip him to live his.

These letters are a culmination of writing I have completed while living in Denmark. Some of the letters were published in various journals, websites and anthologies — and it was never the intention for them to be read as a scholarly endeavour. As I never set out to write an academic paper, the tone of these letters is casual at best, and they move around very much like my mind — back and forth between various themes and subjects. It is not my intention that my son, or the reader for that matter, agrees with everything I set out here. What I do hope to accomplish, however, is to encourage my son to continue his passion for thinking.

I have attempted to structure these letters as much as I could on a timeline, although this is not always the case. I begin with an idea of what pre-Christian Europe may have looked like in order to draw some connections to the indigenous peoples who were encountered in the so-called New World. I also want to say here that although I use the word "indigenous" and examples from the Americas, I think it is important that we recognize that there were great similarities in which Europe met Africa and her people, and that there exists an intersection between what it means to be Black and indigenous peoples.

I have read that many of the Europeans who landed in the Americas felt a kinship with the indigenous peoples, so much so that laws had to be passed to halt intermixing and the Europeans' record-speed abandonment of settler towns in exchange for the indigenous ways of living. Many Europeans, like the Celts, found these peoples' customs familiar — so I am aware that European contact with the indigenous peoples was of course not as black-and-white as is often presented. However, the fact cannot be argued against that it would be one culture that would soon dominate and obliterate other ways of being, and it is this that I am most interested in. As many indigenous scholars and activists repeat time and time again, including the Native American activist Leonard Peltier (quoted later on in this book), the future of the land we currently call America and her people depends on opening up to the wisdom of those who premise their culture, their ways of being on the sacred circle of life. We in the West do not do this and this is, quite frankly, the crux of the matter.

Although there was no pre-European paradise, the unprecedented scale in which European colonisation altered the landscape of the so-called New World is undeniable. Some estimates of the indigenous genocide that resulted from European contact run as high as 75 million. Remember, we're talking about people in the Americas, from north to south and throughout the Caribbean. A recent *Indian Country Today* article on the Anthropocene says:

> No historian seriously questions that the European invasion of the Americas resulted in millions of deaths. The serious debate has been how many millions. What if it was enough millions to change the carbon dioxide (CO_2) content in the atmosphere and therefore the climate and ultimately the

geology of the Earth?[1]

Many times throughout this book, I use our lineage as a narrative and geographical thread to pull themes of race, power, gender and even land rights together. I'm a strong proponent of Audre Lorde's insistence that the personal is the political, or as the sages of the past have pronounced, as above, so below. The micro is the macro and so forth... there is so much separation in this world, and while my opinions on race emphasise our differences, I only do so in the spirit of having to go back in order to move forward. It is true that race is a construct — but one must wonder what good this is as long as social structures still exist that are grounded in the creation of "Black" and "white" and further perpetuate inequality that can, mostly, still be drawn along racial lines.

I touch a little on identity politics, hoping to illustrate how our identities can actually bring us closer together as opposed to pushing us further apart, as some critics claim. We must deconstruct the hierarchical structures of our societies, as well as take various power dynamics into consideration so that we can create new ways forward.

We are socialised to often think in binaries, extremes: good/bad, black/white, etc. I believe the world is lacking in nuance — and by this I mean that there are those who believe European colonialism to have been a necessary step towards progress, while others see it as the very opposite. It is part of my spiritual practice to accept that there is a divine order in this seemingly chaotic world and that rather than lament the atrocities of the past I would rather sift through the carnage for what, from various eclipsed cultures, can be salvaged and help us as humanity, move forward. In my dreams I do like to envision an existence without this current power and social structure that we know in the West. And this vision is important, as envisioning something is an integral part towards manifesting this into a reality. What I think is necessary today, more than ever, is to open ourselves up to more varied epistemologies, to move away from this falsehood that knowledge somehow just sprung up primarily from one region of the world, and that this region of the world is superior to others. It is obvious to me that our knowledge systems are the result of an amalgamation of various cultures and teachings, and it is my belief that when this is recognised and practiced more, there will be more dignity to be had for all students of knowledge, no matter their background. It is said that if a child does not see him- or herself in education, then the education system has failed. A good example of this is the influence that Islam has had on Western thought, which few of us ever seem to learn about.

I've thought about this much as a mother to a biracial child in Denmark and as a teacher. I would like to include a plea for us to wake up and admit that there is a reason why education in the West is structured in the way that it is, and that unfortunately too many of our children are not seeing themselves in the education that they receive. A wise person once said that the primary endeavour of education is to instil in our children a sense of dignity and pride in who they are. From this premise, new worlds can certainly be created, rather than the reproduction of out-of-date knowledge systems and rote learning. Part of the reason why I have written this book for my son is so that he can receive some information that could perhaps balance what he has already learned, or not learned, in school. Unlearning is a tenet of decoloniality.

I've also attempted in this book to connect white settler colonies, such as the US, with Europe, for although Europe likes to cast a judgemental eye on what is the undeniable racism and racist structures to be experienced in the States, I find the lack of accountability and ability to see how this is connected to European expansionism troubling. I hope that this book encourages you, the reader, to see the connections not only between the past and now, but the connections between *here* and *there*. No man is an island, the poet John Dunn has written, "so therefore, ask not for whom the bell tolls, for it tolls for thee." These are fitting words. Right-wing nationalism is not only happening in the States; for the past twenty years or so there has been empirical evidence that similar patterns are at work in European politics. With memories of World War II becoming dimmer and dimmer in the minds of the everyday European, what will there be to remind us of the atrocities to be had from ignorance and bigotry? And what role does this historical amnesia play in the continual control and detainment of Black and brown bodies throughout the West, and especially here in Europe, under the pretence of artificial borders? In this way, memory and history play a big role in this book.

I also hope that it is evident that I am as committed to scrutinising myself as I am to scrutinising countries. Change starts from within — and if there is one thing I can commit to, no matter how faulty I may sometimes be, it is to a life of constant self-examination and, hopefully, improvement. Too often in this world, we expect things to be plastic — unmoving and unchanging, like the glossy pictures in a magazine. But we are dynamic beings, nature is dynamic and people are capable of change. The change that is needed most, however, is a change in consciousness — and I hope this work inspires this.

Lastly, I am acutely aware that Denmark, compared to many other countries around the world, could — as I mentioned in a previously published piece entitled "Conversations in Denmark"[2] — seem like Disneyland. I want to make it clear that it is not my intention to compare Denmark, or the Scandinavian model for that matter, with anywhere else that exists on Earth. I do, however, want to hold up this model to the very idea of perfection itself, as this is exactly how we progress as humans, and not to do so would be complacent and a sign of moving backwards.

Again, you may not agree with some of what I have written here — but at the very least, I invite you to walk in my shoes for a minute in the hope that it encourages us to think even *more*.

The West is not in the West. It is a project, not a place.
— Édouard Glissant, *Caribbean Discourse*

In the Beginning

Dear Son,

Once upon a time, the people of Europe were mostly like every other indigenous group on this planet. They too were comprised of bands of people, who lived close to the land, hunting and foraging — they too understood that nature was not something outside of themselves, but a part of their very being. Women were not necessarily property and the land was not something to be conquered, owned and exploited but something to abide by and respect. It is not my intention to romanticise here. I don't mean to paint a picture that everything was perfect. It was by no means a paradise, but there were aspects that we today could perhaps learn from if we were not taught to wholly dismiss our ancestors as primitive:

> During the Great Forgetting it came to be understood among the people of our culture that life in "the wild" was governed by a single, cruel law known in English as "the Law of the Jungle," roughly translatable as "kill or be killed." In recent decades, by the process of looking (instead of merely assuming), ethologists have discovered that this "kill or be killed" law is a fiction. In fact, a system of laws — universally observed — preserves the tranquillity of "the jungle," protects species and individuals, and promotes the well-being of the community as a whole. This system of laws has been called, among other things, the peacekeeping law, the law of limited competition, and animal ethics. […] It's not MAN who is the scourge of the world, it's a single culture.

One culture out of hundreds of thousands of cultures. OUR culture.[1]

When you arrive in Denmark, one of the most promoted brands is that of the Vikings. But, who were the Vikings, anyway? "Everyone talks about the Vikings," Nils, a Danish captain of the sea, once said to me on the Danish island of Samsoe, "But if it were the brave ones, the courageous ones who left, tell me then, who remained?" he asked, puffing on his pipe. "The cowards," he replied, with a glint in his blue eyes. "We are a nation of those who were too cowardly to leave." We both knew that Nils didn't mean that Denmark was a nation of cowards. What was understood, on the other hand, was how enthusiastic and proud many are to embrace the legacy of the Vikings without fully understanding this past. Well, the Vikings certainly didn't wear horned helmets as so many of us are wont to believe and often buy in souvenir stores here in Denmark. But, if you were to consider the annals of history, you would know about the Viking King of England and the Viking colonisation of the English. You would also learn that the Vikings are said to have reached the so-called New World way before Columbus ever did. It is true that not much is known of the Vikings, and what we do know has come through the Church (which has proven not to be the most accurate recorder of histories). Many theories abound and a quick glance at the Vikings' art, craftsmanship and seamanship will attest to the advanced culture of these people. Clearly, they were not just bloodthirsty, warring brutes. What is often cited about them is that they were fierce sea warriors, slavers and artisans, and, as a recent *Smithsonian Magazine* article revealed, that they included women as warriors.[2] The twelfth-century Danish historian Saxo Grammaticus wrote:

There were once women in Denmark who dressed themselves to look like men and spent almost every minute cultivating soldiers' skills. [...] They courted military celebrity so earnestly that you would have guessed they had unsexed themselves. Those especially who had forceful personalities or were tall and elegant embarked on this way of life. As if they were forgetful of their true selves they put toughness before allure, aimed at conflicts instead of kisses, tasted blood, not lips, sought the clash of arms rather than the arm's embrace, fitted to weapons hands which should have been weaving, desired not the couch but the kill.[3]

How's that for gender equality?

You have tales of the Tribe of Dan, mentioned in the Bible, and there are some who even claim that Scandinavians, the Irish and the Scots all perhaps come from this tribe — one of the original twelve tribes of Israel. Incredible, yes, but it is intriguing to think about. The Tribe of Dan is not mentioned much in the Old Testament, but the references are interesting enough... They were known as a warring sea tribe who left their mark wherever they went. Some claim that this mark is the word "Dan," which can be found in many, diverse geographical regions — such as "Danmark," which is how the Danes refer to Denmark, the Danzig, the Danube, and linguistically everything that starts with "Don," which in the British Isles are abundant.

Indigenous European culture of the past, no matter where you look, had close ties to the earth. Whether we are talking about the Celts, the Picts the Vandals, the Goths, the Gauls — we have been taught to think about these ancient peoples as unsophisticated, illiterate, uncivilised and barbaric, but any half-asleep purveyor of world history will discover otherwise. Go to any museum and check out the work of these people — advanced is more like the word. There is also much evidence, again, that women played no small role in these cultures, with some even suggesting that the patriarchal order came with the bearers of the cross (as is the case with other Abrahamic religions), as Europe and her people were conquered. For, make no mistake about it: Europeans, along with everyone else in the West, are a conquered people.

* * *

One of the most intriguing regional flags I have ever seen is that of Corsica. I became interested in Corsica when I first heard that Napoleon Bonaparte was born there. As a child, I had always been curious about Napoleon and even took a course on "Napoleon and His Age" in my junior year at the New School for Social Research's Eugene Lang College. The professor, a former World War II refugee from Eastern Europe, would punctuate his lectures with comments like, "As I was having coffee with Foucault," and gave us cigarette breaks and lively talks. I thought it interesting that one of the biggest, if not the biggest, of French historical figures wasn't even born on mainland France. I also wanted to learn why he was considered such a historical great. Do you know what I learned? That one of the reasons his troops excelled was because they broke many of the rules of war of the time.

I later became more fascinated about Corsica upon learning that the owner of the cocoa plantation my ancestors worked on hailed from this place. When you look closely at the history of nationhood in Europe, you realise that like everything else it is indeed a construct. The Corsicans themselves, at least historically, know just as much as anyone else what it means to fight for one's sovereignty. When we talk about the European Union, I often wonder — what union? The Germans seem to be in perpetual competition with the French and the British, the

Danes with the Swedes, and let's not even speak about how Southern Europe is looked upon by Northerners. I'm not saying there isn't any love there. What I am saying is that it seems that no matter where you go in this world, groups of people always have problems with other groups of people, and very often, these problems become embedded in legal, social, economic policies. And sometimes the closer these people are to each other, the more heated the contention can be. Let's not forget that in every Spanish election, even up until quite recently, with violent results, the Catalonians consider seeking independence, as do many other nations who have had the discomfort of being ruled by others, such as the Basque. When you look at the history of the UK, for example, you'll see a history of conquest and freedom fights. It could be the English in Ireland, the Scottish against the English, or simply one tribe against another. Now it's nationhood that is the new tribalism. This tribalism shrouds the true mechanisms of power that have been in place since seemingly time immemorial.

Corsica is a small mountainous island off the western coast of Italy, but it is an administrative region of France. If you go through this island's history, you learn that there has been a strong resistance to this relationship — especially since in Corsica, for example, French is not the native tongue, Corsican is more like Italian. I have no idea what brought my ancestor from Corsica to the island of Trinidad, perhaps they were in search of El Dorado but instead found cocoa? I began to read about this country when I learned of this connection that my family has to it. What I found was a flag of a Moorish head — once blindfolded but, after a short-lived independence inspired by Pasquale Paoli, freed of the blindfold to show the brief liberation of the Corsican people.

Why does Corsica have a flag of a Moorish head, a Black head? Who were these Moors who ruled the Iberian

Peninsula for hundreds of years? Although there is an insistence that we are to think of the Moors as Arabs and even as North African, why is the imagery from the past that of dark-skinned people, more resembling what is referred to as even sub-Saharan? Why is the Moor's head Black? Why was he blindfolded? Whose blindness are we referring to? I have never been there to confirm this, but I was once told that there is a motif of this blindfolded Moor's head in the Sistine Chapel. Why don't we learn that much about the Moors in Europe? If there's one thing this image hammers home for me it is that Black people have been in Europe from the earliest of times, and not only as enslaved humans. Noel Malcolm writes about Miranda Kaufmann's book *Black Tudors* in a recent *Telegraph* review:

> A court decreed in 1569 that "England has too pure an Air for Slaves to breathe in"; any former slave who settled here was treated as a free person. Miranda Kaufmann has found records of hundreds of Africans living in England in this period; some were independent, some were servants, but none was a slave.[4]

It hints to our contributions to world cultures — but why is this information so buried? Why do we have to look under the annals of history to find our past? Why do most believe that Western civilisation is Europe, when Europe isn't even a united cultural force as such, but an amalgamation of conquered people, whose histories have been virtually erased and mythologised to the point where these very people accept uncritically this narrative. I ask why? And who does it serve? As a child, I was told through state-issued history books that I, as a young Black girl, did not matter — because, according to the authors of such histories, no one who looked like me ever attained any greatness. Luckily for me I have always been in possession of a fortitude to correct this dangerous erasure and found Queen Nanny of the Maroons, Sojourner Truth, Harriet Tubman and later the three rebel queens of the Fireburn rebellion on St Croix in what is now the US Virgin Islands.

* * *

I started contemplating the sea, stars and trees because, when I did so, the density of politics and social injustices seemed to lighten. When I looked through a telescope and saw the crater-ridden surface of the moon for the first time in my life a few years ago, my own personal struggles seemed insignificant in comparison. Instead, I got wrapped up in the wonder of it — and how little I knew about something that has been there all my life. The moon. I thought about the fact that as a woman, my body had already empirically proven to me that my own reproductive cycle was connected to the waxing and waning of this very same moon. And I'm far from being the only woman who experiences this synchronicity with our lunar friend. In this space of contemplation, I often find freedom.

When I go out to a forest and see the trees and the diversity of life around me, my being becomes relaxed. I get this tingling feeling on the top of my head that opens me up in a way that being in a city does not. I like the way leaves flutter in the wind, the dynamism of nature as opposed to the unmoving concrete of cities. I used to fear forests, nature even, once. Too many fairy tales and movies seemed to root their horror in nature and the unknown, especially for women, and a fear had taken hold of me. But now I know, because I have experienced it, that nature heals.

When I lived in New York, my life was very different to what my life is like here in Denmark. Back in New York, back in the Nineties, I worked in publishing and freelanced for magazines that were built on Black culture. I worked for Marie D Brown, one of the first Black literary agents in New York City publishing, and if you know anything about publishing, well, New York City is it. I met some of the biggest and brightest literary figures sitting in that office in 625 Broadway at Marie Brown Associates. I met artist Faith Ringgold, film historian Donald Bogle and novelist, performer and essayist Arthur Flowers. Marie's office was an oasis for many, no matter the background or profession. Part of my job was not only reading and evaluating manuscripts, writing correspondence and answering phones. It was also to support Marie and the many inter-relationships her presence facilitated. And answering Marie's phone was always like an exciting adventure because you never knew who was on the other end. It could have been Ed Bradley, her best friend and award-winning journalist, whose loss has been a catastrophic one to journalistic excellence, not just for those who knew him personally, but socially and culturally. It could have been Piri Thomas, author of the critically acclaimed *Down These Mean Streets*, or the artist Xenobia Bailey. It could even have been someone calling collect from jail — mostly men whom came to rely on the fact that Marie would talk to them and encourage their writing. It didn't matter because everyone who called Marie's was interesting. Through working there I was introduced to the work of poet and writer Pamela Snead, award-winning poet and novelist Paul Beatty, poet Willie Perdomo, the late great artists Vincent Smith and Tom Feelings and too many others to name.

When I tell people of my publishing background, many express surprise that Black books is a thing. Some want to know why. The answer to this lies in the story of how Marie D Brown came to New York City publishing in the first place. During the Sixties there was a congressional hearing about the lack of Black people in publishing — as publishing, in its best sense, ought to be representative of all people. As a result of this hearing, actions were taken to recruit more Black publishing professionals and to seek out, more actively, more titles representative of this historically overlooked demographic. Marie was one of these people.

Housed in the same building as Marie Brown Associates was Writers and Readers Publishers, along with its many imprints that included Harlem River Press and Black Butterfly Children's Books. Black Butterfly Children's Books published award-winning children's books for children of colour by such authors as Eloise Greenfield and Jan Spivey Gilchrist. Writers and Readers was founded by Glenn Thompson, a literary icon endowed with a strong belief in the transformative power of literacy. He published many of the most talented poets and writers of the time, including Tony Medina, Suheir Hammad, Safiya Henderson-Holmes and Asha Bandele. He also published Huey P Newton, amongst others, and was the creator of the *For Beginners* series, which presented the ideas of figures such as Kant, Einstein, Marx and Darwin in comic-book form. Before beginning these adventures, however, he started a publishing and social-services collective in the UK, Centerprise, in Hackney, which was a successful publisher and cultural centre up until quite recently, when it was closed in 2012 due to a rent dispute.

Glenn Thompson was born in Brooklyn. He and his brother both grew up in an orphanage and Glenn didn't learn how to read until he was twelve. Learning to read for him made a great impact on his life and he dedicated his life to ensuring that intellectual seeds would continue to be sown and that true change could be sparked through the sharing of ideas. Unfortunately, Glenn passed away just four days before 9/11.

Back then my life was split between 625 Broadway, industry parties, catching up with friends, writing or hanging out at the collective where I lived in Williamsburg,

Brooklyn. Sometimes I interviewed writers, musicians and artists such as Paul Beatty, Coolio, Kara Walker, D'Angelo, Gary Simmons and the late Nigerian-American photographer Mfon Essien. Sometimes I met icons such as Chaka Khan, or writer, editor and journalist Susan L Taylor, and even Method Man. In New York, there is always something to do. But despite all of this, I was unaware of the peace that nature would have for me, too caught up in the hectic buzz that is New York. I rarely sat still, my frenetic energy keeping me constantly on the go, barely ever able to live life beyond survival mode. I hadn't realised that I had been running from something and that, one day, it would catch up with me.

When you live in New York, it's hard not to accept the program that you live in the greatest city in the world. Everything is about its greatness: the songs, television, movies and magazines. We even have our own state of mind. Even the most cynical of New Yorkers would have to say, at least once in their lifetimes, that it is the greatest city. You can do anything in New York, no matter what time or day. You want to dance Sunday morning, all day? No problem. Is food your thing? Great! You'll find just about every type of food offered from the four corners of the world there. But even if New York doesn't appeal to your interests, it's still difficult to escape from what must be a billion-dollar industry selling the brand to the world. So, even to the most jaded of us, to even suggest leaving New York can sound blasphemous. But it was spoken about among my circle of friends. One of my best friends in college, Leah (who eventually made it out of New York and now lives on a ranch in Colorado), once famously quipped, "Living in New York is like being in an abusive relationship. You know you have to leave, but can't." New York is far too large to have a singular story.

Moving to Copenhagen, a city miniscule compared to

New York, I realised that I really wasn't cut out for big-city living, although all my life I had thought of myself as the quintessential city girl. I learned that I'm not cut out for the constant bombardment of noise, smells and advertisements... There is something invigorating about city living for sure, but for me, it must be balanced by the spirit that nature engenders.

It never occurred to me that I could create, within my reach, a place to which I could retreat to contemplate, write, clear my thoughts and figure out just where I stand in a world that seems to turn faster and faster the older I become.

Like the cheesy t-shirt says, I love New York, but I also love Trinidad, Maui, Big Island, Molokai, Lisbon, London, Tisvilde, Laguna, Bologna, Venice, Stockholm, Los Angeles, Monterey, Las Vegas, Lanzarote, Mallorca, New Jersey, and I know I will love, just as much, a host of other cities and countries I have yet to discover. For me, the world is simply too big to love just one place. People and cultures are too varied, yet familiar. And no matter how much the perceived differences between groups are accentuated, travelling has revealed to me how these potential barriers can be overcome when we meet one another without fear but on a heart level. It is not everyone who engages in this meeting place, but throughout my life I have experienced that many do.

Living in Denmark has taught me that wherever I go, there I am. It showed me the importance of creating what I missed about New York, here. It hasn't been a seamless journey, sometimes it has even been clumsy, but there have, thankfully, been many successes. What I learned in all of this is that human existence is the perfect reflection of possibility *ad infinitum* and no matter where it is that you find yourself, you must have a supportive community.

I have learned what living your life according to others' values can do to your spirit: it diminishes you, depresses you, because in your heart you know you are not doing what you were truly destined to do: fulfil your dreams, or as you once declared to me when you were ten, "I'm a modelist!"

"What's a modelist?" I asked, suspicious of this word that, although it sounded familiar, I knew didn't exist.

"It's when you live your life the way you want to live it!" And it made so much sense to me.

I have decided to take a step back and perform alchemy. I have decided to step back and create the life that I choose for myself, and you. This is what I have endeavoured to do in the eighteen years I have been here, a country that on the surface seems so foreign to me, yet is so familiar, because in the end, we are all human, no matter the histories that we choose to learn or not.

Diary of a World Citizen

Son,

I grew up with jokes like: What do you call an Indian between two buildings? Ali. What do you call an Indian walking on a wall? Balance-singh. These jokes were not racist — they gave us a way to talk about the secrets coursing through our blood, to claim ownership of a culture that otherwise seemed exclusive but was handed to us through our lineage, our parents and their parents. In Trinidad, everyone knows that if a name ends with "-singh" you are an East Indian, or that you have some East Indian in you. "Singh" comes from the Sanskrit word for "lion" and was originally adopted by certain warrior castes in India. Balbirsingh. It is the name of my mother's family — her father. It turns out the name is Sikh and the prefix "Balbir-" means "strong." Strong Lion. Even though the name is Indian and we ourselves are not a family of Indians, in looking back I can say that it does feel like I grew up in a pride of lions.

Your father once said to me that throughout all his world travels, Trinidad is the only place where he felt he came close to experiencing racial unity. I'm not sure I'd go that far, we do have our racial issues, but anyone who has had any connection to this twin-island nation would be sure to remark on its brilliant and vibrant diversity.

All of we is one, is a famous Trini saying. And our biological offspring are oftentimes a testament to that. There are not too many of us left who, born from the Balbirsingh family line, stay true conservatively to this very Punjabi name. Rather, like so many other families born in the shadow of empire, we are a family of forbidden affairs, courageous love stories that dared to look the establishment in the eyes, and upward and horizontal mobility in a very class-conscious society. Given the colour of our skin, there were undeniable trespasses in the barracks and cocoa estates due to legal and economic constructs based on race.

* * *

When I'm feeling particularly far from home, I often prepare a pot of *callaloo*. Callaloo is a staple Trinbagonian dish, and it is often used as a metaphor for the mix-up that we like to lay claim to. Callaloo is made with callaloo bush and okra — two staples of Trinbagonian cooking — and is often cooked with what we simply call "pepper." Add some crab and dumplings to the dish and it's the stuff *limes* on beaches are made of. The pepper, when left intact, is brightly coloured and about the size of a cotton ball and dangerously hot. You know through me that if ever you see one in someone's kitchen preparations, you don't pop one in your mouth, as a Danish guest of ours once unwittingly did. She begged for us to take her to hospital while we supplied her with copious servings of yoghurt. She survived. Reverence in one's approach to culture is always best.

Growing up in Trinidad gave me a cultural fortitude to add to what I had already received in Brooklyn. While Brooklyn taught me experientially the realities of American racial politics and how to be proud of my diasporic heritage, Trinidad gave me the nail to hammer home a stronger sense of who I am based on where I come from. Black leadership? No problem. I was only ten years old when I arrived at Piarco International Airport in Trinidad with an Afro weighing down my small frame, donning an all-too-large and colourful outfit that stayed true to my Caribbean heritage. I will never forget the comfort I felt when I saw our prime minister. He was brown like me. This was back in the Eighties when most Blacks doubted we would ever see a Black American president.

In the US I learned to be American, but in Trinidad I would learn to be Trinidadian, which, due to its occupied history, was peppered with remnants of British colonialism. Through my accent and ability to "code switch" I unconsciously taught myself the ability to learn another language, which came in handy in learning Danish. It was not difficult for me to learn Danish words such as "de" and "dem" (plural definite article) because in Trinidad we got rid of our "th" a long time ago. Having the cadence of a Trinidadian accent also came in handy in having the ability to sometimes hide my very American one when speaking Danish, something I appreciate as many Danes, when you speak with an American accent, answer you in English! Other cultural lessons gleaned in Trinidad: through Enid Blyton books I learned that Brits said "hols" instead of holiday, and had racist depictions of Blacks called "gollywogs."

I arrived in Trinidad the summer of '82. Although still quite young I had already learned what I had to do to excel in the environment I was growing up in, and for better or for worse, Brooklyn had become a mix of many complex things. While there were double-dutch games and the birth of hip hop, there was also Rikers Island, New York City's infamous 1.672-square-kilometre main jail complex. There were trips to Coney Island and Empire skating rink and the fear and realities of teenage pregnancy. I'd landed in Trinidad after having managed to get kicked out of elementary school. My parents, consumed by the all-too-common immigrant existence of living in survival mode, did the best thing they could at the time: send me *down* there. Back *home*. To Trinidad. I was to become a *barrel child* — that child who lived in her parents' home country, away from her parents to live with family members and not become too American. This stay would be punctured by shipments of barrels, filled with the cheap, material goods of the US like toothpaste and sneakers, things that seemed to take the sting out of Caribbean poverty, distracting us from the greater economic laws at work that crept in between families, seemingly driving us further apart and that destabilized many Caribbean nations.

It was, of course, difficult to be away from my mother. But when I look back on those four years in Trinidad, I am forever grateful for the experience. Without it, I would never have gotten to know my grandparents and my aunts and uncles on my mother's side, and through them, the rich, cultural heritage of Trinidad and Tobago. Thankfully, I was taken under the wings of two girls, both also living in my neighbourhood, Petula Griffith and Joanna Douglas, two girls without whom I would have been completely lost.

I was a not yet a teen when I travelled to Trinidad alone. When I landed and deplaned a thick, humid blanket of air hit me and kinked my hair even more. I loved how the palm trees seemed to relax against the backdrop of the sky. An explosion of crickets filled the air — deafening at first, and soon an imperceptible part of the orchestra of sound that is Trinidad. Sometimes when I would go to sleep at night, next to my snoring grandmother in Diamond Vale, I would think of how similar the sound of the crickets was to the sound of steel pan — an instrument Trinidad has laid claim to inventing: the oil brought money for the rich, and the steel barrels were used to create culture by the poor. And this is what we do: create from nothing, because it is our way.

Stories are Life

Son,

One of my greatest joys right now is being able to witness you as a reader. To see you enjoying something that has been as impactful in my life as reading is truly one of the best experiences I have had thus far on this planet. When you picked up *Don Quixote* to read, I can't tell you how much I relished hearing your thoughts on what is for sure one of my favourite books ever. For me, there is no greater force than story — a force that, under the best circumstances, can inspire change. I was delighted to hear you reflect out loud, of your own volition, on how Cervantes' representation of Muslims seemed to be biased, and at how funny you found the overall tale of Don Quixote to be.

When Patrick Swayze and Keanu Reeves' *Point Break* came out in 1991, I had better narratives than the story of two surfers to dig into. At about the same time, I was sitting in a small West Village classroom in Manhattan pouring over books at the New School for Social Research. Against all my high-school teachers' warnings, I had chosen to attend a small, lesser-known university rather than Brooklyn College, Columbia or NYU, precisely because it was small, located in Manhattan and known for its radical syllabus. I was unaware, however, of what I was walking into, but found my intellect satiated with studies of Marx, Keynes, Kierkegaard and Descartes. It was around that time that I was introduced to Cervantes' *Don Quixote*.

To read *Don Quixote* — in its entirety — and have it taught to you by an impassioned professor who cries at his fate in the end and explains in detail the historical import of the book to the point where you find yourself laughing out loud while reading it, was like landing in literary heaven. An enthusiastic teacher is infectious, and she was successful in instilling in me (and everyone else in that class) a deep appreciation of Cervantes' masterpiece. I love that Quixote is this guy who was really into books about knight-errantry and that he was so into it, that it was all he did... read books about knight-errantry... so much so that one day, he was convinced that he himself was a knight errant. And so off he went, through his garden, out through his gate and astounding/confounding all those he met with the idea of who he believed himself to be. To him, Rocinante was the most gallant of horses, while to others he was a sack of bones. How could you not fall in love with a character so in love with his own vision of the world? That to me is the pure genius and power of a strong narrative. How much are we affected by what we read? Before movies there were books. Before books, oral tales. Narrative is important. We learn vital lessons about life through story. And my story back then was... well... yes, it was *Don Quixote*.

At about this same time two young men in Copenhagen were bitten by Patrick Swayze's *Point Break*. They decided after watching the movie to go to Hawaii and learn to surf. Yes, just like Don Quixote. They decided to go out into the world of their dreams and be surfers. Unlike Don Quixote, this was not simply a matter of walking through one's gate and out into the world declaring, "I am a knight surfer." This meant working, saving up the money, exerting discipline in order to execute a plan. They did it, and a year later they went to Hawaii.

What does all of this have to do with you?

One of the literary programs I attached myself to quite early was that of James Baldwin. I found his books, dusty with age, in my Uncle John's collection of classics in his home in Diamond Vale, Trinidad. My Uncle John was a man typical of his generation from the Caribbean: well-versed in the canon of Europe and of Amílcar Cabral. You have met him, when we all travelled to Trinidad many years ago, but you may have been too young to remember. He was once the secretary of state, during Dr Eric Williams' prime ministership in Trinidad. Dr Williams wrote the seminal classic *Capitalism and Slavery* during his time at the University of Oxford, and was our leader once Trinidad and Tobago gained independence from Great Britain back in 1962. This government, despite the disappointment it would later prove for many, was unique because of the promise it contained, the cream of Trinidad and Tobago's intellectual crop: and my uncle was one of them.

Although my Uncle John was quick to joke that my father was from behind the bridge (a ghetto in Trinidad), there was one thing that formed an affinity between us, and that was books. We connected over V.S. Naipaul, Vladimir Nabokov, Earl Lovelace and Sam Selvon. It was the power of books that united us, and finding a copy of *If Beale Street Could Talk* in his collection, and later learning everything I could about James Baldwin, instilled another narrative in me: that of the Black expat writer. Like Don Quixote, I decided that I was a writer, although it would be years before I walked through my grandparents' rust-chipped white gate on Emerald Drive to embark on this journey.

As you already know, your father and his friend, Tue, did go to Hawaii. Through a collection of humorous experiences they have shared, as tales of adventure, they learned how to surf, ducked the shade that native Hawaiians are infamous for throwing foreigners (if you know their history you understand why), got tans and even witnessed anti-Black racism while in the US. After their stint in Hawaii they were ready to return to Denmark. But before Copenhagen, they figured, must be New York.

Fast-forward to me graduating. It is the evening where the writing majors are to present excerpts from the novellas they were required to write to pass the course. The Atrium is a beautiful room on Eleventh Street right off of Sixth Avenue. It is across the street from the college I had just spent four years attending, learning about everyone from Paulo Freire to Michel Foucault. I am reading from my work *The Mothers of Memory*, and in walk two very blonde and tanned Danes.

* * *

There's a lot more to this story, but the seeds to a new narrative were sown. But which narrative would it be? Once, some years after you were born, when our new family of three were sitting on a beach in Maui, as we looked out to the horizon, your father said, full of wonder, "What must it have been like to be on those ships sailing towards these islands, seeing them for the first time?" Without skipping a breath, I chimed in, "I wonder what it was like for the inhabitants of these beautiful islands when they first saw those ships coming towards them, forever altering their world?" And there you were, barely four years old, sitting between us, the sand in your little brown toes, a manifestation of that bridge between the world of your father and mine.

Although we were worlds apart in culture, there were specific things that united us: reggae, a love of travel and a curiosity about life. Your father introduced me to the healing qualities of nature. I slowly shed my big-city fear of sleeping in tents, and one of my best memories will forever be camping with you both in Hana on Maui. It rained all night and there was a hole in the tent. And while you and I slept soundly through the roar of the flash storm, your father remained awake, dumping the water out of the tent.

Through your father I met the old-fishing village of Tisvilde — off season, the best time to be there. When you were a baby, we would camp throughout Denmark and in Sweden, where there is every man's right to camp. Your father and I also both had pets called Iggy: his was a rat and named after Iggy Pop, mine a cat named after Ignatius J. Reilly — from *A Confederacy of Dunces*, one of my all-time literary favourites.

As you of course know, we did not remain together, but there is one thing that does: my respect for him. It's not often you hear someone speak highly of their ex-husband. And in an attempt to put healthier narratives out there that perhaps can seed some more positivity, I have to admit that the integrity of your father is the stuff that greatness is made of.

Thank goodness for *Point Break* and the hopeful dreams of two Christianshavn guys. If not for that perfect combination I wouldn't have had the biggest treasures in my life: these are of course you, and fulfilling my lifelong literary dream of living life abroad.

* * *

I first arrived in Denmark via train from Paris and pulled into Copenhagen's Main Station as my point of entry. As the train entered Copenhagen I remember seeing a huge mural of what appeared to be a beautiful "African" girl. This image that greeted me, outside of its cultural context, seemed dignified and devoid of any of the usual racial stereotypes I have come to expect, unfortunately, from Europe. I had not yet known about Denmark's colonial past, and as it turns out her eloquent image is used to sell a brand of a coffee here, and is called *Cirkelpigen*: the Circle Girl. I must remark that at no time have I ever seen the image and thought it to be anything other than a mature woman, not a girl. But again, I had no context in which to view it at the time, other than what I already had with me, and so she, drawn unbeknownst to me by a Danish artist, came to symbolise a hope I had of Denmark that began on that day. Looking back now, after eighteen years of living here, I understand how this hope was perhaps unrealistic, as I had hoped that by coming here I could escape the dense racial ignorance that can be a brutal reality in the United States. And while I have been successful in this, to some extent, I have had to face the harsh truth of what Baldwin meant when he said that America comes out of Europe.

When I first arrived in Denmark, I couldn't find anything that challenged the dominant narrative and so in 2007 I started my blog, Blackgirl on Mars. Through this blog I was able to meet a resistance, albeit small, of artists, activists and scholars who challenged the silencing and erasure of Black voices. Artists such as the Jamaican-Danish artist Michelle Eistrup, through projects such as "Not about Karen Blixen" (which insisted on a decolonial dialogue with the work and culture around Blixen), would create works of resistance that hoped to ignite other ways of understanding our collective past. In 2015 the Danish newspaper *Information* published an article titled "Have you forgotten why it's called colonial goods?" ("Har du også glemt, hvorfor det hedder kolonialvarer?"), in which Mathias Danbolt, an assistant professor at Copenhagen University, wonders about Denmark's colonial nostalgia — something evidenced in everything from the now discontinued "African head" candy to, again, the Circle Girl.[1] This is, of course, all a nod to the times when Denmark had not only colonies in the Caribbean, but also a presence in Ghana and was in the business of kidnapping and selling indigenous Africans. Denmark, I would learn, like most of Western Europe, built her fortune and country on the blood and tears of indigenous people from Africa and the so-called Americas and everywhere else she took her imperial project, only to

30

profit immensely from the impoverishment of said colonies. This movement has gained more traction throughout the years I have been here, and includes, but is not limited to, art historian, creative educator and postdoctoral researcher Temi Odumosu; Iranian Danish writer Nazila Kivi; Norwegian Eritrean video artist Miriam Firesewra Berhane Haile; the Sweden-based Eritrean scholar Rahel Weldeab Sebhatu; Inuit writer and artist Aka Niviâna; and Swedish-Trinidadian researcher Michael McEachrane, to only name a few. Through the Danish Trinidadian artist Jeannette Ehlers I was introduced to Dominican German curator Alanna Lockward, whose BE.BOP (Black Europe Body Politics) 2012-2018 brings together activists, visual artists, filmmakers, writers and scholars on the idea of decoloniality, such as Swiss Haitian artist Sasha Huber, Robbie Shilliam, Dutch Mexican Rolando Vázquez, the Dutch Surinamese artist Patricia Kaersenhout, Danish poet Mette Moestrup, Quinsy Gario, performance artist and researcher Teresa Maria Diaz Nerio, Walter Mignolo and countless others, too many to list.

* * *

There's a great scene in Monty Python's *Life of Brian* entitled "Before the Romans things were smelly." It's one of their most cited scenes and the entire point is that the People's Front of Judea (a group of revolting Jews) are plotting against the Romans and the question comes up: "What have the Romans ever done for us?" The joke, of course, is in the answer, which is not singular but reveals the many advancements and improvements that Roman occupation and domination had supposedly brought to Judea such as the aqueduct and sanitation. I bring this scene up because every so often there is the opinion expressed that colonisation is the best thing to have happened to Africa, the Americas and everywhere else Europe has made her mark. But what this argument excludes is the cost of these so-called advancements: the continued genocides, the kidnapping, the ethnocide, land and resource theft.

In January 2016 an *Independent* article declared, "British people are proud of colonialism and the British Empire."[2] The article cited a YouGov poll that revealed that 44% of the people polled believe this. There could really be no other explanation other than the colonial amnesia that Europe promotes that ensures that her citizens remain ignorant to the death and devastation that European colonisation meant for many of my and others' ancestors. Of course, 44% of people would think colonisation was a good thing if they did not learn the truth in school and if said colonisation improved the pockets of their country, and thus its development.

* * *

But as I sat on the train from Paris to Copenhagen, I was not thinking about these things. I discovered that going through Germany was much like driving through New Jersey — it was huge and never seemed to end. The train was old, with thick, polyester curtains undoubtedly made before the Eighties, and the train car smelled like cigarettes. When I heard the conductor, a German woman, yell for the tickets, I was reminded, lest there be even the slightest chance I'd forgotten, how far from Brooklyn I was. This was not my first time in Europe. I had visited Amsterdam a few years prior to this with an old friend Reggie, but it was far from what I was doing now: travelling alone from one country to the next.

Paris had been all that I had envisioned: I stayed at a hostel where I was awakened by the bells of the Sacré-Coeur. I ate cheese and baguettes. I hung out with a man from Martinique who played the guitar and sang Bob Marley songs and whose Polish girlfriend made me *pierogies* for breakfast. While I travelled with luggage, I met backpackers from all around the world, some of whom I'm still in contact with. The World Cup had come to France that year and festivities were in the air.

I shared a train compartment with a Nigerian man who was in the Norwegian army. He was tall, beautiful and chatty and perhaps that's why I forgave him when he said, "The problem with Scandinavians is that they're not particularly clean." I rolled my eyes and chuckled *why were humans always going on about the cleanliness of those deemed foreign?*

When the train pulled in to the station, I said goodbye to my Norwegian soldier. I was told to meet my Danish host, Tue, your father's travel companion to Hawaii years before, "under the clock" — the most popular meeting point in the station. When we met up, one of the first things he told me was that we didn't have far to go but — get this — that there was no shower in his apartment! I couldn't help but laugh. I asked about it and was told that whenever I needed to bathe, I would have to use the public showers at the main station or at the many swimming pools in the city. I smiled inwardly, remembering my Nigerian travel companion's assessment.

However, the absence of a shower in an apartment, I would learn, was of course not due to any cultural uncleanliness but to the fact that many of the apartments in Copenhagen were, at that time, still old. When I first arrived here, it was not uncommon to find an apartment with a toilet that was in the backyard, or shared by many apartments on the same floor and with no hot water even. For an American, where big is everything, this of course strikes one as strange. While I've had apartments in Manhattan with bathtubs in the kitchen, these were the exception, not the New York rule. I had arrived in Copenhagen at the beginning of a gentrification process that seems to follow me wherever I go; and the city continues to be modernised, with luxury harbour apartments and a conductor-less metro to connect this small city at integral points. And like every other Western city, affordable housing in Copenhagen is becoming increasingly hard to find.

Although I'd met your father before arriving to Copenhagen — years ago in New York when he was returning to Denmark after spending two years in Hawaii — this would be the trip that meant you.

* * *

I fell for your father on a sunny day in Enghave Park. I believed, and to some extent I was right, that connections could be forged between Danish writer Dan Turèll and Toni Morrison, the Rolling Stones and hip hop. I was right, for a while, especially since it was the music of Sade that seemed to mediate. When I had arrived in Copenhagen, your father and his crew of friends, mostly all from Christianshavn, received me warmly and dedicated themselves to making me feel welcome. Many were children of what seems to be a quickly disappearing socialist sentiment, a sentiment that appears to have been swallowed up by this nation's allegiance to a more neoliberal agenda which has seen cuts in social welfare and less compassion for those deemed socially weak. I felt welcome, back then, and the only irritating aspect was every now and again meeting a Dane who thought they had me figured out because I was "American." You see, there were some people who could not imagine that I may not have been what their stereotype of an American was, although my loud voice begs to differ.

I rode around Copenhagen on your grandmother's bike and, if it was not available, on the handlebars of your father's. I remember how beautiful I thought Copenhagen to be and how relieved I felt that I could see the sky, uninterrupted by what seemed to me the gnarly mechanical teeth of tall buildings, biting into the heavens in New York, creating breathless skylines, while at the same time swallowing up the sky. I felt a calm wash over me in Copenhagen — something I could never feel in New York.

Your father, chatty and knowledgeable about the city of his birth, was an excellent tour guide. I liked that he was a conscientious consumer and was knowledgeable about the world. He is as much as an outsider as I am, to some degree, and in that we found a path. We both enjoyed Hemingway, Steinbeck and Al Green. Through him I discovered the beauty up north. Although I had lived in Trinidad for some time, I had never made touching base with nature a part of my life routine. Like too many other New Yorkers, I rarely travelled upstate or to any of the other beautiful surrounding natural spaces in New York, except, of course, Central Park. I'd been to the Hamptons once during college, but it was an uncomfortable venture away from home: my friend's family were obviously surprised to see me in a *Guess Who's Coming to Dinner* kind of way. My friend would later confess to me, in annoyance, about his parents' relief when they learned that we were not dating. He told me he had never seen "that side" of his parents before. The only other Black person that weekend was the woman who cooked and cleaned the house. I was shocked by how rigidly segregated it all felt — but it would not be the last time that I would find myself in such spaces either here in Europe or in the States.

You'd be surprised how many of us who grew up in New York have never really seen the New York countryside. My parents were too busy trying to stay afloat to arrange visits anywhere upstate, and outside of one childhood bus trip to Bear Mountain I wouldn't really see the more rural New York until I was an adult and in my forties. When I visited

Woodstock, I was surprised to experience that where I was did not seem much different than being in Scandinavia or the segregated US south.

I liked how quiet Copenhagen and her countryside were compared to the New York I was familiar with. By this time, I had grown weary of the hustle and bustle but had not yet connected this to the necessity of having more of a balance in my life. Living in New York you come to attach yourself to the vibrant pulse of the city. Denmark has brought me closer to nature, and by being here I have learned to listen more to the stories told by the landscape and the water. This, my son, has saved me by providing a space for me to heal and grow.

When Terrorism Has a White Face

Son,

Your father and I created a family and we made a small, cold-water flat in Vesterbro our home. He ensured that the pine-wood floors were sanded and cleaned and I have to admit that despite the truant splinter or two, it did look beautiful. We lived a very simple life with a futon mattress as a bed, sarongs as curtains and decided not to have a television — which of course changed on one of my mother's visits. ("I want a television!" she groaned as though she could not live without one. Lucky for her the very next day I found one in the garbage.)

Your father made simple and tasty meals like burritos and veggie burgers, and we spent a lot of time, the three of us together. While he worked, I stayed at home with you. You were an easy baby to mind. You were happy and slept well. I spent my time watching television (thankful that in Denmark they use subtitles and do not, like the Germans or French, dub their television shows and movies), knitting you sweaters, reading, taking walks with you and meeting up with other new mothers. I have to admit that back then it was sometimes a challenge for me to leave the house, as I felt very self-conscious about being a foreigner in Denmark. The anti-immigrant rhetoric began for real when I had arrived although everyone assured me that, "You're American! It's not you they're talking about!" As if that should have comforted me.

Marrying someone from another country might sound exciting, but the bureaucracy that oftentimes comes with it can be stress-inducing. At about the same time I moved to Denmark, the government experienced a shift in its immigration policy, making it more difficult for Danes to bring their foreign spouses to make their homes in this country. Although the restrictions were not as tight as they now are, it still meant that for the first four months of my pregnancy I was unable to be a part of the healthcare system. This however, was remedied by a team of intrepid midwives who created a secret network to ensure that foreign mothers received the prenatal care necessary to ensure healthy births. This taught me that despite the harsh anti-immigrant rhetoric and stringent immigration laws, not every Dane was prepared to overlook their humanity.

In a recent *Business Insider* article entitled "The Nordic countries are the worst in the world for making friends, according to expats," the findings of InterNations' recent study "Expat Insider 2017" were revealed. The study asked more than thirteen thousand expats about quality of life in sixty-five different countries.

> Norway, Denmark, and Sweden take up the bottom 3 places for finding friends. More than six in ten expats find it hard to build friendships with the distant local residents. "As in most Nordic countries, people are quite private, closed, and… not that open to conversations with new people," said one British expat living in Sweden.[1]

As Martin Amis says, "The first thing that distinguishes a writer is (s)he is most alive when alone."[2] This is true, but loneliness, especially on foreign land, can seem even more of a heavy burden to deal with. We are all alone, in the end, they say — and living in Denmark has helped me deal with this universal truth a bit more authentically, I suppose, than if I had remained in the States.

But in the end, nothing could ever make up for the fact that I am a mother, away from my own family, navigating life in a foreign land. There is a mourning that must happen, a reckoning with both the past and the present, to push forward. Sometimes I shudder when I think about what the experiences must be of those who do not have the privilege of Western citizenship. Of mothers who have fled war, who cannot speak eloquently in the language of empire, whose educations get erased by biased criteria.

As I mentioned before, it wasn't too long after I arrived that Denmark started to turn up the debate on immigration and, although folks told me time and time again that it was not *people like me* (translation: "You're not Muslim") who were being targeted, I couldn't help but feel uncomfortable — I mean, if someone could be targeted in a society as Muslim immigrants were in Denmark, then that meant *anyone* could be, as far as I was concerned. In a recent article in *The Conversation* entitled "Scandinavia: the radical right meets the mainstream," Mette Wiggen writes:

A legitimisation of radical right-wing ideology is taking place around the world. The world was shocked by the events in Charlottesville, America, and by [45's] failure to condemn racist violence. But it may be even more surprising to some to learn that the radical right has achieved a mainstream foothold in Scandinavia and the right-wing parties and groups have been accepted as legitimate and part of the mainstream. [...] In Sweden, the Sweden Democrats (SD) is the second-biggest party in the polls, despite its fascist roots. Parties such as SD owe their success largely to their stance on immigration [...] The Danish and Norwegian parties are more established and more professional than most of their European sister parties and have long been accepted by mainstream political parties.[3]

As someone who has spent a great part of her life studying history — particularly how it is related to race — I would be remiss if I did not mention that it should be apparent to all that white supremacists are in governments all over the Western world.

Despite this glaring truth, in the many years that I have had the privilege of living here, I have experienced the hesitancy there is to talk about race in Denmark. This reluctance, unfortunately, has meant that progress in a collective understanding of how the past impacts the present is relatively slow-moving. This however, does not mean that there are not folks who want to learn.

Recently, I was contacted by a Danish director who had decided to do a puppet show for kids about Danish colonisation. However, it all seemed to go wrong when on one of the first days of the production, the only child of colour in the audience, a young biracial girl, began to cry. I was recommended as a consultant and the script was sent to me to review. As I read the piece, it became clear to me why this young girl felt so sad. The play was faulty not in its intention, but in its execution, as it was full of racist stereotypes and an oversimplification of the kidnapping and enslavement of Africans and the role it played in advancing Denmark and her people. There was nothing to make a young child of colour feel good about him- or herself. The imagery and story only further reproduced hierarchical notions of race. In further discussions with the director and actors, and after seeing the play a couple of times, the theatre decided to stop the production of their own volition. What I most appreciate with this situation is that they could tell something was wrong — and they did not run from this because it made them feel uncomfortable. The experience was an enriching one for both the theatre and myself. Throughout this job, the Danes expressed to me frustration at how little they knew about this period of Danish history.

I was pleasantly surprised at their determination to better understand the historical variables at play and their openness to hearing where they could do better.

I was moved by their insistence to get it right, and pleased that they did not silence and dismiss my review. Yet the experience illustrated to me once again the uncomfortable truth of the so-called privilege many have of never having to consider race because their own lives have never been directly impacted by it (or at least they are not aware of how). I was made to realise, yet again, how many only equate overt acts of racism as racist as opposed to the subliminal ways in which it is often reproduced; and how insidious yet seemingly innocuous acts can abound in white spaces, rarely to be challenged because very few ever consult people of colour. There seems to be an idea in Denmark that racism is a thing that only happens in the US — not something that exists here despite the tacit acceptance of the white norm.

I once got in a conversation about race with someone, a white woman who was the mother to three Black children. "You're always talking about race!!" she said to me, somewhat annoyed. I was confused. Her response and volume of her voice did not match the conversation I thought we were having. "You are the racist, Lesley, you are the racist, with all your talk about Blackness!" What!?

In Denmark, folks love to say, "I don't see race" — but what about the others? What about the thousands of children who live here and who must deal with the violence of erasure every day? Who deals with public debates discussing how much they are accepted (or not) in the society in which they find themselves? And what about the fact that when we don't talk about race, we end up talking only about whiteness? Luckily for me I have met many Danes who want to reach a better understanding of this issue. But in the trickster world of white supremacy, people like me are labelled racist. This is the genius of "the death project": turning all on its head and emptying words of their true meaning.

In *Race, Rights and Rebels: Alternatives to Human Rights and Development*, Julia Suárez-Krabbe writes:

> Following the lead of the indigenous Nasa people of Colombia, my understanding of the death project refers to the exercise of violence in coloniality, which targets the actual processes of life and the conditions for existence: in short, plurality. The Nasa describe the death project as such: "The conquerors brought with them their death project to these lands. They came with the urge to steal the wealth and to exploit us in order to accumulate [wealth]. The death project is the disease of egoism that turns into hatred, war, lies, propaganda, confusion, corruption and bad governments."[4]

I want to make clear that I find little difference between these situations that I have experienced in Denmark and what I have experienced in the US, or Trinidad and Tobago, even, when it comes to white supremacy and racism. Sure, Trinidad and Tobago is comprised mostly of people of African and East Indian descent, but you would be hard-pressed to find someone of European ancestry living in the ghettos there. The only difference is that here in Scandinavia, the population has managed, through a tacit policy of erasure, to keep relatively insulated and ignorant of the ramifications of empire and colonisation.

Sometimes this inability to confront the elephant in the country can be exhausting. This is when Denmark's countryside offers me respite. Whether it was in Tisvilde, where we'd spend a lot of time when you were a baby, or in the many other spaces of green that can even be found in this magical city, I would return to her — mother nature, to bask in the soothing energy that is her. Whether it was in the small wooden house named "Amigo" that your father spent his childhood summers in, with its pot-bellied oven and nearby forest with paths to the seaside, or being able to pick herbs from the garden, like lemon balm, and make tea, these are the things that I learned comfort me, sustain me and fortify me.

It was in Tisvilde that I truly learned to appreciate the basic offerings of the Earth and that I would never stop learning and adapting to practices that are healthier and more life-sustaining.

One of my earliest memories is being with my grandmother in her garden in Diego Martin, a suburb of Port of Spain in Trinidad. I remember revelling in the wonder of an okra which I had picked. I remembered looking at the emerald green fuzzy skin and breaking it open to find that it was a pentagram, encasing little pearly seeds. I fell in love that day, and was delighted when I later learned that the world "okra" was the same as the word for "soul" for the Akan people of West Africa. According to them, the okra is the very essence of god in all living things. I also was once told that the plant made its way out of Africa when an enslaved woman hid the seeds in her hair. This love and connection to okra and to a large extent plants would be interrupted by inner-city living and all the trappings involved. But I always attempted to get back to the land, albeit intermittently — whether it was in college when I worked on an organic farm in New Hampshire (and learned how conservative this northern state could be!) or continuing to assist my grandmother in her garden when I lived with her as a child.

Being in Tisvilde in your early years provided the calm I needed to read, write and knit. And mother. Whenever the weather allowed it, we were there, usually your grandmother, you and I — and when your father got off from work, he would often join us. It was like we were the spokes of the wheel that all radiated from you, and I experienced first-hand that it truly takes more than one person to raise a child. My compassion for single mothers grew — and I realised what an almost impossible task it is to do so single-handedly. I'm not saying that it can't be done — I'm just saying that, based on my experiences, extra support is helpful and ensures that not only the baby's needs are met, but also those of everyone else involved in the endeavour of raising a human, including the mother.

Like many other new parents, your father and I were both freaked out by the gargantuan task parenting seemed to be. Your father often wondered about the consequences of raising you in the city, albeit such a small one. He longed to leave Denmark to return to Hawaii. He wished for you to grow up with sun, the sea and close to the Earth. He had also grown tired of the anti-immigrant vitriol that was beginning to become normalised here.

Son, the image is mightier than the sword. An image communicates at the speed of light. No matter which civilisation you look at, the first writing was done in pictures. This is why imagery such as Holland's Black Pete and even the imagery in Djurs Sommerland here in Denmark is so upsetting to many of us. These images reproduce a power structure that was born out of the enslavement and general debasement of our ancestors. It denies us our humanity and teaches the next generation, albeit subliminally, of a racial hierarchy that many wish to remain unchallenged.

With every expedition that Europe sent to the so-called New World, there was always an illustrator. An illustrator? Even our ancestors understood the power of images in usurping our conscious power — if one is not aware. An image imprints itself unto our subconscious, often declaring itself to be *truth* more instantly and directly than text on paper.

Expeditions are peculiar things. They were sent out to

survey the land, subdue the people and subsequently expand and so enrich the empire. To gain control of that territory, so that enterprising kings and peasants alike (although not too often the latter) could amass fortune and so power, they needed to get the support of the people back home. They had to make conquest more palatable. It is not difficult to imagine that much of the imagery created to be sent back to Europe was not a true reflection of who these people were. For some of us take for granted that "human" is a universal concept, but we also understand that the word, when created in a colonial context, did not extend to us, or white women, for that matter (just as the term "universal" did not contain us either).

What if I told you that Europe, or at least some involved in these early expeditions, even Christopher Columbus, already knew of the existence of these people? What if I told you that human beings, way before Columbus, were communicating, sailing and trading with one another? I mean, is it a coincidence that Columbus set sail not too long after the Moors were defeated and kicked out of Spain? When do we begin to see the connection between Shango, the god of thunder for the Yoruba, and Thor, the god of thunder in Nordic mythology — which, by the way, was the actual spiritual belief of the Vikings? When do we begin to see the connection between all Earth-respecting people, despite the wars (which benefit a few) of the death project? That the influence of what we regard as knowledge and wisdom is global, if not *pluriversal*. You, a studier of history and fast at logic, would proclaim: "But what is new about this knowledge?" You would say that by now, as mentioned previously, mainstream science is pretty much saying that the Vikings were in North America before the Spanish, and you may even be so advanced as to say that Africans were in the Americas, even before the Europeans. I mean, Thor Heyerdahl lived his entire professional life showing that it was possible for early humans to navigate the seas using simple floating devices made with thatched reed, not to mention all the sophisticated craftsmanship demonstrated by the Polynesians and the people of ancient Mali and Egypt. But the problem here is that this is not taught in schools. Too many of our institutions of learning insist on archaic, singular interpretations of history that deny the pluralistic nature of the world. And so what we often miss, even possessors of this knowledge, is the next logical step. And that is that very few people, too few, are aware of the fantastic interconnectedness of humanity — for to do so would unite us as opposed to perpetuating the compartmentalised historical narrative that is taught in too many schools.

Race, my dear son, is a construct, they say. And it certainly is. It was constructed to justify the enslavement and subjugation of people that was necessary to Europe's death project. It was constructed to create a class, a class upon whose labour all other labour would be based. An erased class, whose stories continue to be buried by the tales of the very people who enslaved them. It is true, historically speaking, that calling oneself white or Black is a relatively new affair. In a recent *Aeon* article entitled "How 'white people' were invented by a playwright in 1613," Ed Simon writes:

> The Jacobean playwright Thomas Middleton invented the concept of "white people" on 29 October 1613, the date that his play *The Triumphs of Truth* was first performed. The phrase was first uttered by the character of an African king who looks out upon an English audience and declares: "I see amazement set upon the faces/Of these white people, wond'rings and strange gazes." As far as I, and others, have been able to tell, Middleton's play is the earliest printed example of a European author referring to fellow Europeans

as "white people". [...] The scholar Kim Hall explains in *Things in Darkness* (1996) that whiteness "truly exists only when posed next to 'blackness'" [...] Hall explains: "Whiteness is not only constructed by but dependent on an involvement with Africans that is the inevitable product of England's ongoing colonial expansion." As such, when early modern Europeans begin to think about themselves as "white people" they are not claiming anything about being English, or Christian, but rather they are making comments about their self-perceived superiority, making it easier to justify the obviously immoral trade and ownership of humans.[5]

As we've talked about before, many people don't even dig using the terms "Black" or "white," finding them inadequate adjectives to capture the depth of who they feel themselves and each other to be. But racism is not dependent upon individual beliefs in its power. No. When there are systems in place that are rooted in the idea that land can be owned, and that one group of people can own another group of people, it cannot so easily be dismissed — especially when these systems are ripe for abuse in the hands of people who are either unaware of the historical processes that have brought us all to this present place, or perhaps don't even care to know. As the *New Oxford American Dictionary* states,

Although ideas of race are centuries old, it was not until the 19th century that attempts to systemize racial divisions were made. Ideas of supposed racial superiority and social Darwinism reached their culmination in Nazi ideology of the 1930s and gave pseudoscientific justification to policies and attitudes of discrimination, exploitation, slavery and extermination. Theories of race asserting a link between racial type and intelligence are now discredited. Scientifically it is accepted that there are subdivisions of human species, but it is also clear that genetic variation between individuals of the same race can be as great as that between members of different races.[6]

Why is it that Westerners have carte blanche in terms of borders, but those from the vestiges of empire do not? Why is it that a visa to travel to most countries in Africa is a relatively possible affair if you are European or American, even, but travel the other way around is so controlled? It is historically irresponsible to insist that race does not still play a large role in how we see and relate to each other.

The reason illustrators were included on these early expeditions was because there needed to be someone to create the imagery for what Europeans would come to learn to be the "New World." In a time where there were no cameras, having someone on hand to manually reproduce what was being seen, or what they wanted you to believe was being seen, was important.

Now, remember, this was pre-industrialised Europe. Most on this continent were, let's face it, living pretty much under oppressive conditions and were not as civilised as many of the nations that would be destroyed by them. Most territories had been Romanised by now — Catholicised — and people were burning at the stake. Heretics, they were called. An Abrahamic religion wielded its iron fist and made Man king — and women? To paraphrase Zora Neale Hurston, "Women are the mules of the world."[7] These societies were burning "witches" at the stake at a horrifying rate. Some reports claim there were villages all throughout Germany where not a single woman or girl could be found. This happened over a span of *hundreds of years*. Who were these women, girls and sometimes men? As many historians have noted, there is a connection between this femicide and the genocide that would be enacted in these foreign lands, the genocide that was necessary in the death project, the ushering in of a racist, capitalist and misogynistic order. Capitalism is founded on racism and misogyny.

The expeditions that were being sent out were representing certain interests — the interests of those who sponsored and invested in them. The investors of these ventures were usually crown men — and knew already of the vast amounts of wealth to be had from the land and her people. The opportunities trickled down, of course, which is what galvanised Columbus, the son of a weaver, to embark on his exploration to begin with. He wanted to be Admiral of the Sea, and he was, for a minute. We cannot forget that Columbus began his career on the western coast of Africa. Tell me son, what do you think he traded in? Do you not think it odd that a murderer and human trafficker is so revered by the powers-that-be?

We all know what went on to happen. That we learn. We learn about the genocide and the extermination of the indigenous people of the so-called New World, the kidnapping and enslavement of our ancestors from Africa. But how could it have been allowed or even accepted?

The illustrator held the power in his tool. He could tell narratives through his depictions, he could transfer these people's humanity, or not. He could portray these people as kind, humble and subservient, or even deviant. If the imagery is negative, it impacts all who see it, conveying messages to the soul about who these people are represented as being — not about who they truly are.

There are numerous accounts, from Columbus himself, that suggest many of the people who were encountered were in fact cultivated, intelligent and peaceful — civilised. There are accounts that testify that many of these people did not even raise a hand to their children — because it cannot be supported that the way to mould a child's soul is through the rod. Many had cities more advanced than those in Europe at the time and, judging from the few accounts that reach us from the conquered people themselves, they were cleanlier than their European murderers.

But still, wars were waged upon these peaceful people and the people subdued. How could this barbarity, slaughter, have happened? Those of us who care much about this narrative often wonder. And I say that this was partly accomplished through image — an artist's interpretation that failed to convey the humanity of the people depicted. Along with this strong and influential arm of PR, these men also brought with them European diseases, which the indigenous people they encountered were not immune to. Between these new diseases and the violence of the Europeans, by some estimates, the indigenous population of the Americas fell by as much as 130 million from 1491 to 1691.

There's a saying in Trinidad that is used when someone acts in a way that is selfish and not community-oriented, as if they are better than someone else. When someone's aunt fails to appreciate the creative tongue borne from Africa and whatever European language they have found themselves living under ("pidgin," it is incorrectly and derisively called) someone else responds, "What happen to she? She feel she white, eh?" This proclamation, this charge, if you will, comes from the experience of having foreigners, such as Europeans, come into your country, dismantle your community, disregard your humanity, all in the name of a supposed humanity. *She feel she white* speaks to this imperial arrogance. The current European anti-refugee sentiment is ironic, don't you think?

Race is a product of European imperialism. Race will be no longer useful when there is no reason for hierarchy and capital, when life begins to be valued, when the Earth is respected. We need those who have descended from a race of people and who think that they are solely responsible for all things considered enlightened, cultural and progressive to wake up to this reality, this new Earth. We need those whose skin looks like the earth to protect the Earth.

* * *

Sometimes I want to leave Europe and go home. But, dear son, where is home for me? Is it the Brooklyn where I was born, but which no longer exists as communities continue to be pushed out through a new form of colonialism, now called gentrification? Is it Trinidad and Tobago, a place in which I have not lived since the late Eighties? Son, after much thought it is, in the end, where you are. And why should it not be? Why should I feel that I have any less of a right here, in Denmark, or Europe even, due to the colour of my skin? As the poet and urban geographer Teju Adisa-Farrar proclaimed in one of her recent tweets, "We live here. We exist and always will. And oh, just so you know, We Are Staying."[8]

When you were three, your father, you and I, travelled to Hawaii in the hopes of escaping the xenophobia that had begun to infect Denmark. But we returned after only six months. I didn't like that we were so far away from family — especially since you were so fond of your grandmother, your father's mother. You two have always shared a strong bond and I'll never forget that as soon as you started to talk, you called her Nana — which coincidentally is common in my culture. How could you know this? I remember how your grandmother's face beamed the first time she heard it and said, "I like that, he can call me Nana." How could we take you away from this?

Returning to Denmark, believe it or not, was a relief for me. By the time we had the money together to travel to Hawaii, I didn't want to go. I didn't want to pick up and move halfway around the world again — and this time with a baby. I was exhausted, and just wanted to stay put. I'll never forget how sick you were the evening before we were to leave. I didn't think we should travel. But against my better judgement, we travelled with you, and all throughout the flight, you coughed a cough that didn't sound too right. We travelled through New York and once we arrived in Brooklyn, it didn't take us long to have to bring you to Brooklyn Hospital — and after a string of misdiagnoses you finally started to feel better.

But in the beginning, it didn't look good. You were listless and I thought I was going to lose you. How can I describe this feeling? This feeling of powerlessness a parent feels in the face of a grave illness of their child? I became sick as well — and had been diagnosed with pneumonia. Luckily, we had health insurance and could seek medical assistance. There are so many others in the States who do not have this right, this privilege. Remember, in the US it's your right to own a gun, but not to have health insurance. We tried everything the doctors told us and although you broke out with a rash on your body, the doctors never mentioned meningitis. You had gotten a shot right before your illness — and for years later, you would scratch yourself on that spot where you were given the injection. Not one single doctor mentioned that it could have been an allergic reaction to aluminium.

Finally, you started to get better and we continued our journey to Hawaii. But when we moved back to Denmark and you would later be diagnosed with a severe hearing loss, as parents, we could not rule out this period of acute illness we had experienced you suffer. What really happened to you in New York? Was it meningitis? An allergic reaction to your shot? It is frustrating that, as parents, we will never know.

So we returned to Denmark six months later. I didn't like having to leave you with strangers in Hawaii whenever we needed a babysitter. I also didn't like how blatantly Hawaii seemed to be colonised. Sure, there are many who say that

Hawaii has benefited from being a US state. But tell me, why is it that the indigenous people seem to have benefited the least from the presence of multi-national corporations and the US military? The indigenous Hawaiians that I met during my time there were intensely proud of their heritage, as they should be. There was, as is always the case with occupation, talk about sovereignty — an investigation of the history of these islands will reveal a history just as brutal as any other in the colonised world. No amount of US dollars could ever erase this. An interesting aside is that both in Hawaii and Denmark the word "sovereign" is used as slang to denote something good.

When we returned, we signed you up at a Waldorf day-care that bussed you out of the city every day and took you out to the forest. I signed up for Danish classes and started the process of learning another language. Much to Denmark's credit, these programs of integration are provided and are certainly better than nothing. But something was amiss. You kept on getting into a lot of fights, and the day-care leaders would joke that it must have been because you were born in Brooklyn. "He wasn't born in Brooklyn," I would tell them, afraid that you were already being pigeonholed. Finally, and thankfully, the leader had a question for us. "Have you ever had his hearing checked?"

We thought we had. When I first arrived here the birthing services were first-class, at least compared to the US where companies are not even required to grant maternity leave to expectant mothers, who instead must settle for "sick leave", with as little as two weeks off, if any, coupled with the fact that this leave is not anywhere near close to the time one receives in Denmark. Some of the services that were available to me included maternity classes in English and being assigned my own midwife (called a *jordmor*, a word that translates to Earth Mother, how beautiful is that?). Some of these services still exist but unfortunately there have been many cuts. One of the services that is still provided after giving birth is having a nurse visit you, at home, for the first few weeks/months to ensure that you and your baby are adjusting to life. They weigh your baby, talk to you and, among other things, check the baby's hearing. However, the hearing test, which has since been eradicated due to its inefficiency, involved ringing a small bell. The child's hearing was judged on his or her response to this. Turns out that's the worst possible hearing test you could give a baby. Babies are so hyper-alert that they usually respond to most stimuli. You had passed this "test."

With the assistance of the day-care leader, you underwent a battery of tests through which we discovered that you were severely hearing-impaired. And then it all came flooding back to me: how you would mouth my words as I said them (so you taught yourself how to lip-read). In your first few years of existence on this planet, you were always close to me. I breastfed you, and so it seemed natural that I had always had you nearby. But now there seemed to be another reason for this connection. It didn't help that you learned quite quickly to say "bye-bye."

You were three and a half years old when you were diagnosed. You may not remember this, but you and I were elated. You never resisted your hearing aids, experiencing immediately the improvement upon your life. We put up pictures of other hearing-impaired children in your bedroom. I know that using hearing aids has never meant that you hear like all the other kids. It just meant that it gave you a perspective that in the end, I know made you and continues to make you a stronger person. I don't think anything happens without a reason. I've never had that luxury.

Your father, however, didn't take it so well. Looking back now, I'm sure it was a combination of having to return to Denmark from Hawaii — but also, as he expressed it, the fact that he had, like so many other fathers around the world, had a dream for you. His dream was that you would be involved, like him and my father, in making music. I told him not to worry, that your deafness could never limit you in anything you set your mind to. And you have proven me right. For the past few years you have been making beats. You currently go to music production school and have even sold some of your beats around the world. You have already in your short life here on this planet shown that everything is possible once you put your mind to it and have, as many children can do once their parents are listening, reminded us how important it is to follow your heart, and to create ways where before they seemed to be none. That is our way.

This is no small feat in a country known for *Janteloven* — that credo that Danish society (but is certainly not limited to Denmark!) is said to be premised on:

o You're not to think *you* are anything special.
o You're not to think *you* are as good as *we* are.
o You're not to think *you* are smarter than *we* are.
o You're not to imagine yourself better than *we* are.
o You're not to think *you* know more than *we* do.
o You're not to think *you* are more important than *we* are.
o You're not to think *you* are good at anything.
o You're not to laugh at *us*.
o You're not to think anyone cares about *you*.
o You're not to think *you* can teach *us* anything.[9]

A credo which can be said to be of the stuff that stifles dreams, prevents many from reaching for the stars and, most importantly, encourages all to accept their social standing. They say that Denmark is a classless society — and compared to many other countries, it does appear to be so. However, if one were to peer carefully just below the surface, it does not take long to see the difference between those who live in Gentofte municipality, where the local public school for kids is called "the mink farm," and a public school in Nørrebro.

* * *

In going over these events, it is startling for me to discover how soon your father and I split after our return from Hawaii. When I look back now, I realise that during all of this, I had also received the news of my father's death not too long after we returned to Denmark. The last time I had seen him was when we were on our way to Hawaii — and he had been living in a home close to Brooklyn Hospital. Somehow, I knew, as I hugged him, that it would be the last time I would be doing so. He seemed so angry, so sad — and I felt powerless in his wake and, an adult now, unwilling to be consumed by his temperament.

I go so fast sometimes — and now with the privilege of all the time that has since past, I can see how the stress of becoming a new parent in a foreign country, your father's and my decision to move to Hawaii and back again, the death of my father and the later diagnosis of your hearing all had to be dealt with somehow. To be sure, there were other things at play as well, but I would be remiss and dishonest if I didn't take the time to say that I wish I had the clarity back then to at least handle things differently. But I didn't, and the next best thing I can ever do is to learn from these experiences, and take them on and to continue to strive, always, to be a better human being and parent to you.

Things go so fast sometimes.

… I wish to slow down.

What Whispers the Water?

> We need to dig and jump into the land we come from;
> one woman after another, one dream upon the other,
> calling up who we are.
> — Ntozake Shange

Son,

All my life I've been curious about those in our family who came before me. Like so many other children, I was born asking questions: Who are we? Why are we here? But as the descendant of a colonised people who were forced to forget their own beginnings through violence, and of a family who came to believe all that empire had taught them, the answers I received were not designed with the intent of empowering little brown girls. As a child, I was greatly disappointed by the answers given to my questions by the adults around me. From the existence of the patriarchal god that was given to me, to the inequalities in gender and race that I had witnessed as a child, it appears no one around me was equipped with any satisfactory answers. I was to understand, however, that children were to be seen and not heard — something I resisted with every breath in my body. In this quest for truth, I picked up reading quite early and discovered alternative ways of being, knowing and living.

I have always had an innate sense that it would be through digging up the stories from the past that I could gain some understanding of life and would so be helped on my way forward, which in turn could push us, more collectively as human beings, off this path of self-destruction that we so evidently seem to be on. Son, we are inventive people, conjuring up paths when others have been denied. What others have attempted to erase is still with us; the waters, if we are still, whisper our stories.

* * *

We, son, are island people.

From the twin nation of Trinidad and Tobago to Manhattan and Brooklyn on Long Island, Maui, Zealand in Denmark, islands have always been a part of our lives.

What is a baby in her mother's womb, if not an island, surrounded by the natal waters that speak in a language of memory? Water is time past, present and future, it *is* memory, it is thought, it is dreams. And I wonder what it was that was whispered to you, as you grew in the darkness of my womb, surrounded by the water of all waters? What are the stories that were told? Were they stories about loss? Of the joy I felt on learning I was carrying you in my womb? Were they stories of my mother, my grandmother and even those who came before? Did you hear the voices of our ancestors? Your great-great-grandfather's cry when he entered the world on a boat destined from Chennai to Trinidad? Was it the cries of our kidnapped ancestors from Africa, or the joy of those travelling of their own volition, making paths between this continent and others? Was it the Corsican? Did you hear him? Or the childhood rhymes that I would sing on the pavement in Brooklyn, along with other little brown girls with colourful beads in braids, breath smelling like bubble-gum and singing not-so-innocuous children's rhymes such as:

Rockin' Robin, tweet tweet tweet
Rockin' Robin, tweet tweet tweet
All little birds gonna' really rock tonight

Tweet tweet tweet
Mother's in the kitchen cookin' rice
Father's on the corner shootin' dice
Brother's in jail, waitin' on bail and
Sister on the corner selling fruit cocktail
Rockin' Robin, tweet tweet tweet

Or was it the blues of Nina Simone? The soca of Sparrow, the calypso of Lord Kitchener or even the jazz of your namesake Thelonious Monk? Did you hear your grandfather's playing on his Hammond B-3? The jams that I grew up with in Brooklyn, comprised of Trinidadian men, all arriving to Brooklyn with hopeful hearts and the ability to blow a trumpet, play the conga or strum the guitar (but not necessarily possess the ability to survive on this new, foreign terrain)?

Memories whisper to me, from the ocean, through the mist, the wind. It seems fitting that I am here, on the Danish island of Anholt, to write this letter to you. As you know, the kingdom of Denmark — your birthplace — has over four hundred islands. One can say that Anholt is shaped like a bird, a dipper even, and it lies in the dead centre of Kattegat, an ocean that has its own stories, its own histories; surrounded by Sweden, Zealand and Jutland.

It is summertime in Denmark and the weather has been reminiscent of when I first arrived in 1998 — grey and windy and cold. I would quickly come to learn the Danish adage, "There's no such thing as bad weather, just bad clothing." Anholt, the island on which I am now, has a terrain a bit similar to Tisvilde. It takes twelve hours to drive to Anholt as opposed to the couple of hours it takes by train to get to Tisvilde from Copenhagen. I love to travel by train throughout Denmark and Europe, and I especially like the journey to Tisvilde. Particularly that part of the route when the small train, *grisen* (the pig), goes through Gribskov, one of Denmark's many forests. Back in the day, the train was old and I found the sound of its loud engine comforting. Back then, Denmark seemed to be a quaint trip to the past — but alas, no country is an island, and all nations, no matter their origins, will benefit from an honest reckoning with their past, present and future. But this, of course, rests heavily on the willingness of the people to interrupt their *hygge* — that culture of cosiness that has even the Anglo world peddling its benefits to their overworked and underpaid North American and British counterparts. It makes sense that *hygge* is such an institution here given that workers here are so much more protected than in other places in the world. With socialised healthcare and free education (with even private education being subsidised by the government), it makes sense that we can afford to value time with family and friends. And as a friend of mine recently reminded me, it isn't free! We pay for it with our taxes! I think it's safe to say that there would be no *hygge* if not for the social welfare system and the higher standard of living that some claim stems from Denmark's colonial past.

I do want to take the time to note here, however, that even with Denmark's strong social welfare programme, things have become more and more challenging for many Danes, and *hygge* for more and more people is becoming increasingly not so easy to come by. Along with Denmark's relatively recent love-affair with neoliberal policies have come extreme cuts to social welfare programmes, a "pull yourself up by the bootstraps" mentality, along with a strong belief in non-existent "trickle-down economics." As you know, I have often taught English courses to many of Denmark's largest corporations, and I have met many fatigued and stressed workers who are fearful of losing their jobs. It is this fear that is harvested by the right-wing parties who convince the populace that it can all be blamed on immigration, a rallying cry so absurd when one considers the miniscule percentage of immigrants in this country to begin with. Xenophobia is fuelled by bad economies.

* * *

I didn't travel through Denmark to get to Anholt, however. Instead I flew on a tiny ten-passenger airplane from the former capital of Denmark, Roskilde, and in about forty-five minutes landed on a small runway scattered with grass. Whenever I have the privilege to travel at leisure like this, with the spirit of adventure, I tend to have more patience, and thankfully, have only had positive experiences travelling throughout this country and the rest of Europe. My experiences in Denmark are even more positive now as I know the language enough to get around. And even if my language fails, I often find that most are all too happy to help.

If you're a foreigner, it's not that difficult to walk away from the news with the feeling that you're not wanted here. With the country's second-largest party being right-wing nationalist, Denmark is indeed at an interesting juncture in how she sees herself in relation to the past, present and future. Considered a leader in maintaining Fortress Europe, how Denmark moves forward is of major importance in relation to borders, migrations, asylum, wars and how it all relates to the rights of freedom of movement.

When I arrived at the small airport in Roskilde, I spied a young couple. An interracial one. They were both Danish, and as they leaned into each other and expressed their attraction to each other in the awkward way the newly-in-love do, I felt comforted by the young lady's confidence expressed in her laughter, her well-put-together clothes and apparent obliviousness to others. She didn't fit the bill of what some would say a Dane looks like, but rather defied and challenged the view, like you. The pilot, a man named

Rasmus, was friendly and once seated on the plane passed a plastic container full of liquorice — that Danish staple which usually I detest — but for some reason I took one and, for the first time, enjoyed. Maybe whether one likes liquorice or not should be the qualifier for Danish integration and citizenship?

Anholt has a similar terrain to Tisvilde, but there are some differences. The forest is full of a variety of trees endemic to Northern Europe — spruce, birch, beech and oak. Although both islands have had a history of wandering dunes (Anholt has the only designated desert in Europe), Anholt seems to be heavily populated by scots pine — a tree whose leaves contain even more vitamin C than citrus fruits do. Tisvilde also has lots of pine and is blessed with an abundance of rose-hip bushes, everywhere from its beaches to people's gardens. Rose hip too is full of vitamin C and I particularly like the jam that is made from it.

The house in which I am staying in Anholt once belonged to an award-winning Danish art director who no longer has memory. The house, on loan, is made of wood and is replete with the seemingly omnipresent Poul Henningsen lamps, a pot-belly oven, and the type of knick-knacks common to summer houses such as glass buoys hanging from the ceiling and an array of life-like objects made from branches, stones and feathers. I later learned these figures are *gryle* — trolls who live out in the desert here in Anholt and are known to cause mischief — and a creation of the man who once lived here.

The house's smells of sun-dried clothes, pine and a slight mustiness remind me of Trinidad, Hawaii, Woodstock, New York and a wooden cabin I once lived in in Lutsen, Minnesota.

As I write this you are at the summerhouse in Tisvilde with your father. It has been years since I last visited. Gilleleje, another town on the northern coast of Zealand, is where I spent most of my time when I was pregnant with you. Gilleleje is the location of Søren Kierkegaard's favourite spot, and when you sit and look out into the Kattegat you cannot help but feel the connection to this ancestor of Denmark. I hope that you go there one day. And if you do, know you were there once in my womb, as I sat on the very spot in which he sat, and looked out into the very body of water upon which he too once did. I wonder what the waters whispered to him?

I have been blessed here in Denmark regarding your father's family and the various people I have managed to meet and work with in the political and creative sphere. Not that long ago I was invited to a public school in the town of Nivå where I spoke to the ninth-grade students about colonisation. I was together with Garba Diallo, the founder of Crossing Borders, a Danish organisation that promotes intercultural understanding. Through my poetry and other writing, I often get invited to various schools throughout Denmark to speak about colonisation, where I use the story of my family and the history of Trinidad and Tobago to illustrate the many nuances and perspectives of European colonisation. I was truly moved by the students' engagement and interest. They were overwhelmingly Danish, with a young lady of Turkish descent and a young boy from the Congo being the only two non-white students in the class. Despite this, or perhaps because of this, the class took an active interest in our presentation. I was particularly impressed and hopeful after this experience. It is always beautiful to experience students who meet you with warmth, openness and interest in learning. I say this having had the experience (seldom, true, but still an experience) of adults who are incapable of letting go of their own personal defensiveness when faced with the task of acknowledging history from others' perspectives.

As you know, I have done quite a lot of work here in

the eighteen years that I have been here, with the hopes of facilitating a more open dialogue on issues such as race, gender and migrations. I have people in my life who I trust and who are committed to breaking the patterns of oppression that are all too often repeated, even in spheres of supposed resistance. I have managed to take you with me to Trinidad twice, and we have both been to Berlin, Barcelona, London, Nice, Cannes, Venice and Bologna, among others. Although life has been challenging here, I would be remiss if I did not acknowledge how my American privilege has opened doors for me. Life has been good to me here, and it is in this spirit that I would like to declare that these letters are not only to you my son, but to the country of your birthplace. I hope that there is something useful that can be mined from these pages, not just for you, but for the people whose country I have lived in for over eighteen years, so that in these challenging times, we can move forward in a more pluralistic way as opposed to the mono-narrative and erasure that is so typical of our current knowledge system.

As they say in Trinidad, "What doh kill, fatten," and certainly my tenure here in Denmark has been boot camp for the soul. There is no better way to confront yourself and the world than in a foreign country, and life, my son, must be examined. I too must examine myself, as I insist on examining history and the geographies that have been etched in my memory through lineage and travel. I too possess the coloniser in my veins, in my body, my mind. I too, must undergo a rigorous introspection that requires that I reckon with the internalisation of colourism, racism, classism, misogyny and sexism.

Who taught me to love myself?

* * *

What stories does the water tell? What stories were

64

whispered to you when you were in my womb? Did you hear your grandmother, my mother, teaching me to sew flowery doll dresses as I sat on her lap on our leopard-print couch in Brooklyn? Did you hear my grandmother's laugh, bubbling forth, when I was a child and, after seeing her naked, asked her where could I buy a vagina like hers? Did you hear my father as he guided me through *E G B D F* and told me how in Trinidad the notes are designated by the words *eat good bread dear father* and how this would end up being such a profound piece of advice for him in the years during which he would succumb to his demons (perhaps the wrath of our forgotten ancestors?) and, like so many children of empire, fall to the parasite that infiltrates our economic, social, mental and spiritual systems?

* * *

Where the political landscape of the world tends to depress me, the countryside speaks a language to me that is soothing and healing. I am stronger now, but part of my journey has involved a mental, spiritual and emotional *dis-ease* that can unfortunately be a part of facing the legacies of being a product of European colonisation and all that has meant to colonised people the world over. Post-colonial stress syndrome. This includes the anxiety of being around people who think that there is only one narrative. This includes the rage of having strangers invade your personal space and put their hands on you in public places. This includes the violent omission of your ancestors in history books. This includes, for too many, consistently being held out of traditional employment opportunities. This includes the continual racist imagery and language that European power seems to be so dependent upon and that so many are so unwilling to let go, for to do so would usurp whatever ideas of supremacy some so desperately hold. on to. Add to this the general ignorance and blatant racism that seem to have boomeranged with a much darker and almost imperceptible force the world over, along with living *far from home*, and you can perhaps understand a bit the darkness that seemed to have washed over me. But, as one of Denmark's most famous writers Hans Christian Andersen once advised, going into the darkness is necessary to find the light. Denmark, with her sunless winters, has given me enough darkness, and I have now found the light, which you are such a big part of. It is in the darkness of the Earth's soil, after all, that seeds take root and grow. It was in the darkness of my womb that your life was ignited and so unfolded. It was in the darkness of the heavens that the universe too was sparked. And for this I am thankful. For nations can be about the people, for sure, but nothing is more universal and encompassing than the land herself. And it is in the land, the earth, no matter where we are in the world, that we will always find salvation.

We live in what can be viewed as perilous times. Our planet is getting warmer at an unprecedented rate and migrations will only continue to grow as the children of former empires are left to deal with the climatic consequences of the industrialism their ancestors and land were exploited for. Hurricanes that are born in the Sahara travel the same routes that our enslaved, brutalised and kidnapped ancestors once sailed. Many claim this is no coincidence. Borders are tightening and US federal departments are censoring the use of the term "climate change." But there are solutions, son. And many of these solutions can be found outside of the parameters that are currently in place:

> Scientists and farmers around the world are pointing out that we can regenerate degraded soils by switching from intensive industrial farming to more ecological methods — not just organic fertiliser, but also no-tillage, composting, and

crop rotation. Here's the brilliant part: as the soils recover, they not only regain their capacity to hold CO_2, they begin to actively pull additional CO_2 out of the atmosphere.[1]

I once read that the land in Denmark is among the most over-farmed in Europe — the land, like its people, is in need of radical healing. We, the children of Earth, must heal, because whatever we have done to the Earth we have done to ourselves. There are those who believe that the land is on loan from our descendants, and there are those who believe that they can rape the land and her resources. There are those who know that there is enough on this planet and there are those who say that there is not enough.

Politics is all about power — and it is not politics that will save us. All you have to do is find yourself surrounded by the wrong activists to learn that there is a difference between those who are fighting for a piece of the pie and those who want to prepare an entirely different dish. There are those who understand that, although it may seem that the sacred has been perverted and that words are devoid of meaning, we live in a world that is still full of wonder and power. You will soon learn, son, if you have not already discovered this, that it is not gender, sexuality, nationality or the colour of skin that will bring people together. To paraphrase the British filmmaker Isaac Julian, you cannot tell someone's beliefs or politics by the colour of their skin, nationality or even sexuality. No. But I will tell you about "meeting places" — that place where you connect with someone else, that space where your interests intersect — and how once you become clearer and focused about your purpose, these "meeting places" can be cultivated into art and action. You will find that the best way to learn about someone's character is through the work that they do and not only how they treat you but most importantly how they treat those perceived to be the *weakest*.

But you know this. You told me the other day about what you found to be the most frustrating aspect of your hearing impairment. You said you just couldn't stand people who acted like you were stupid because you asked them to repeat themselves to you. While I cannot say that I can ever understand what it means to be hearing-impaired in this world, I am pleased that you see it as a filter. These are the people that you don't need to waste your time on. And while we're at it, I want to take the time to commend you for your attitude when you were telling me this story. I love your confidence, son. I love your humour.

It is on this island of Anholt that I am reminded of the beauty here in Denmark. Like Tisvilde and Gilleleje, Anholt too is an old fishing community ravished by the overfishing of industrialised food production. However, these are booming tourist attractions now and the harbours show very little signs of distress. On the contrary. One can still feast on langoustines, shrimp, cod amongst holidaying Danes, Germans and other mostly Northern Europeans.

* * *

Ultimately, though, we cannot talk about liberation, son, without talking about the land, and as our bodies are made from the very stuff of the earth, I encourage you to look at your skin and not only to decode the book that is written there but also to remember that we are, and always be, children of this universe. No country, no border, no war, no law should ever be allowed to infringe upon this sacred tenet. And in those moments where you may seem to forget, I urge you, son, to make your way to any of the many harbours or coastlines that surround us on Zealand, and look out to the water. Ask her, what whispers the water? And be still, so that she can tell you.

Brooklyn Is War

Yes, and the body has memory. The physical carriage
hauls more than its weight.
— Claudia Rankine, *Citizen*

Son,

Sometimes the war a child is born into is not that of a
country, but the one in her own home. Her father is an
irate man-child dictator; her mother, the domestic prisoner
who ensures that his power is never challenged. This child's
and her siblings' bodies, the river whose movements must
be controlled, must be dammed, prevented from going their
own, natural course. Sometimes the very people who are
supposed to protect you end up doing you the most harm;
sometimes a child's birth is not welcome — her presence
makes demands on the adults around her that economic
realities won't facilitate and besides, how much do you think
a little brown girl is worth, anyway? This is the transference
of oppression. This is how abuse reproduces itself. This is
how seeds of trauma are planted, like landmines sitting in
your body undetected until something happens. Something
triggers it and you explode. Again and again. Generation
after generation… until we return to the land, to the waters,
and listen to her and so use this wisdom towards our own
liberation. We are told that we are separate from nature.
Our culture seems to be anti-nature. We eat her, take from
her and attempt to subjugate her. But we *are* nature, not
distant from her.

They say that architecture determines behaviour and I

often wonder: What behaviour does the infrastructure of modernity lend itself to? What is the benefit to be had from living in boxes, often one on top of the other as so many buildings in cities around the world are fashioned? And even more importantly, what behaviour does the housing that is often relegated to the poor inspire — from the projects in major US cities, to the council estates of Europe? Tell me son, what do you think it inspires?

* * *

Here is a conundrum about life: The longer we live, the closer to death we come.

* * *

Our bodies remember that which our minds cannot. The aches and pains that visit us remind us of issues not faced and if we are lucky, if we are in a space where we can dismantle the pain, we can stare our demons down and, like the rebellions of enslaved Africans of old, burn them down with the cleansing power of fire. "Slash and burn" is how the cane fields were worked. Slash and burn: clear the land, start anew.

* * *

2017 was the hundredth anniversary of when Denmark "sold" what are now called the US Virgin Islands — the islands of St Croix, St John and St Thomas — to the US which, interestingly enough, never did endow its inhabitants with the right to vote in the US. Imagine that — an entire population with very little electoral power. Usually Denmark has been slow to understand its historical past but this year something interesting happened: a resistance organised itself around this commemoration. It was a resistance that was composed of scholars, artists, curators, musicians and dancers, among others. I wrote a few stories for the Virgin Islands' newspaper the *Source* which were to be an account of the on-the-ground goings on over here in Denmark. The Virgin Islanders wanted to know: how was Denmark marking this occasion?

One of the artists from the US Virgin Islands who I was privileged enough to meet and interview was the Crucian La Vaughn Belle, who coincidentally also has roots in Trinidad and Tobago. Belle's work is often manifested as a graceful resistance to colonial thought and celebration of her lineage. It was Belle and Trinidadian-Danish artist Jeannette Ehlers who first introduced me to the four queens of the 1878 Fireburn and the "Queen Mary" folk song:

Queen Mary, oh where you gon' go burn?
Queen Mary oh where you gon' go burn?
Don't ask me nothin' at all. Just give me the match and oil.
Bassin Jailhouse, ah there the money there.
Don't ask me nothin' at all. Just give me the match and oil.
Bassin Jailhouse, ah there the money there.
Queen Mary, oh where you gon' go burn?
Queen Mary, oh where you gon' go burn?
Don't ask me nothin' at all. Just give me the match and trash.
Bassin Jailhouse, ah there the money there.
Don't ask me nothin' at all. Just give me the match and trash.
Bassin Jailhouse, ah there the money there.
We gon' burn Bassin come down,
And when we reach the factory, we'll burn am level down.[1]

Fireburn was a labour protest for workers' rights and labour reform primarily in the sugar industry in 1878, and although it took place on St Croix, was the first labour rebellion in Danish territory. It was in response to the inability of the formerly enslaved to earn a liveable wage. The protest was led by four women, Queen Mary Thomas, Queen Mathilda Macbean, Susanna "Bottom Belly" Abrahamson and Axeline "Queen Agnes" Salomon, all of whom were brought to Denmark and housed in a woman's prison until they were tried. The woman's prison, according to Jeannette Ehlers, is the building Christianhavners call the Layer Cake House, and which houses the bakery of the very same name. How ironic that a building that housed some of our most revolutionary heroes now hosts one of Denmark's most renowned bakeries? It seems that wherever colonisation is concerned, the business of sweetness has always been a bitter one. Ehlers and Belle are currently in the process of creating a Queen Mary memorial sculpture and project and intervention to this recent hundredth-year commemoration of Transfer Day.

* * *

What is it in my life that I have had to slash and burn, so that new life could spring forth?

* * *

There is a ringing in my left ear that happens every so often. When I was ten years old I had already grown tired of my father's capricious dictatorial ways. We never knew what would set him off. There was no rhyme or reason to his rages. I was often beaten for doing things I was never taught not to do, but that he somehow felt like I should have known. Things like saying "Good morning," or, "Excuse me." My lessons in this were physical ones. Where once my greatest fear was getting *licks* from him with one of his leather belts, by the time I was ten I had grown bored and defiant of his predictable unpredictability. He had already successfully passed his rage down to me. A rage I would re-enact on the streets of Brooklyn, getting into fights in school playgrounds and in other parts of the neighbourhood. I was developing a reputation and fearlessness that would eventually get me kicked out of school in the fifth grade.

"What were you doing outside?" your grandfather demanded from me when he came home from work early and found me outside, jumping double-dutch with my neighbourhood friends. I'd thought he had gone to work and so I had snuck outside to play. There I was, my skinny ten-year-old self standing defiantly across from my father in our living room in the two-bedroom apartment on the sixth floor that we lived in on Ocean Avenue. Many of the children back in Brooklyn had to claim the front of buildings as our playgrounds. First kisses, games of double-dutch and gossip all took place on these concrete pavements. I knew my father was going to hit me — I had disobeyed him. When I answered that I had gotten permission from my friend's mother to go outside, I was met with a resounding smack on the right side of my head. I temporarily lost my hearing. 'Til this day, every so often, the hearing in my right ear sometimes seems to collapse into itself and produce a loud, ringing sound. Whenever it does this, I return to that day, standing in the living room, right outside our messy kitchen, full of empty Guinness Stout bottles and unwashed dishes. And although my father has now been dead for some years, he appears to me alive and in full view, his anger faltering in the face of a rebellious child now defused and cleansed by the ritual of his passing.

There is an anxiety that still visits my body. It is the anxiety that would devour me when my father got into one of his rages and I knew that licks were headed my way. "Everybody does get licks in Trinidad," my mother would explain when I questioned my father's disciplinary methods for offences as slight as walking in front of a television without saying,

"Excuse me," or walking in my mother's high-heeled shoes for fun. I felt so betrayed by my mother, who would silently sit while my father unleashed his rages on us children. I wonder how much of this anxiety I have passed on to you? I wonder how much of this I have inherited? Science says we carry within us the experiences of fourteen generations, and if we were to roll our lineage out is it the anxiety of our ancestors driven out by a British-imposed impoverishment in India? Or is it the anxiety of our ancestor Baboolal being born on a ship from what was Chennai en route to the island of the birth of my parents? Is it the anxiety of our ancestors on the Corsican-owned cocoa plantation in Todd's Road and the violations this could have facilitated, the births that would eventually come but could never be talked about? Is it the anxiety of our ancestors packed tightly into ships, of being kidnapped and whipped? Or just the anxiety of my own father on the receiving end of corporal punishment turned norm at the hands of his own mother? "You think this bad?" he would ask, as I cried and rubbed the wounded skin on my body after one of his rages, "You should see how it was with my *mudder*. She would beat me with whatever it is she could find!" Perhaps it is even his own mother's anxiety, from being thrown out of her house, pregnant and sixteen, and with no place to go? Or perhaps it is the anxiety of the World Wars, both I and II, which although they took place in countries far from Trinidad and Tobago still impacted the availability of food, played a role in the disappearance of sons and daughters sent to war for empire, and would necessitate the presence of foreign military on our shores and ensure an entire generation would express their food anxiety through hoarding, like my grandmother once did? A recent *Smithsonian Magazine* article claimed that "your childhood experiences can permanently change your DNA."[2] How has our DNA been changed as a people?

Maybe it's all of this, coupled with the anxiety of our

ancestors who were in Trinidad even earlier, who made their way north from what is now known as South America, on the Orinoco, making their way up the Caribbean islands, only to be forever interrupted by the genocide that would befall them with the coming of the Genoese, his men and disease?

Yes, some women are islands, capable of sustaining life. When I carried you in my womb, what were the memories whispered to you in the waters of life? Were they of the pain of the women I come from? Were they of the secrets of shame that have tied tongues and hearts into knots of silence, that have been translated into prayers to saints (the ancestors of others, and so further emptying us of any knowledge of where we are from, and who came before us)? It may seem that the greatest loss with European empire was the erasure of our ancestors. But a beautiful fact in the law of life is that as soon as you start speaking to spirit, she speaks back. And your heart becomes engaged in your life and you begin to realise that our ancestors have never gone away — they have always been here, waiting for us to call their names, breathe life back into them, to conjure up their powers. And son, this is powerful. What Earth is asking for, now more than ever, is ritual. Imagine what would happen to Earth if we humans focus our energy on healing her — she would be healed. Healing, individual, collective, Earthwise — is the order of the day, the common denominator in all that is colonial oppression and exploitation.

I'm certain, too, there is the memory of me, in childhood, giggling with love as I follow my childhood friend India and her mother Willie-Mae into their Buick Destiny, where we would drive down Ocean Avenue to Coney Island to visit their family. Through them I would experience and learn the beauty and tenacity that is the African American spirit, raised on southern soil, now seeking refuge in northern cities. I hope you see me, my skinny nine-year-old self, hanging outside my building, mouth red from Now & Laters, out of breath as the neighbourhood kids play RCK (run, catch and kiss). Fall is in the air, summer has slipped away, and all the lucky girls wear plastic jackets with roller skates on the back, some with hair delicately braided with intricate patterns that once told our ancestors about secret passages to freedom.

Not only did we lose the land but the land lost us. The Americas, and all other places subjected to European colonisation, are stolen land. No amount of talk of democracy and Western freedom will ever alter this.

As a child in Brooklyn, I would often wonder who was there before us? Before the tree-lined concrete pavements, the brick buildings and endless streets. I always wondered what Brooklyn would look like without all of this... about the land that was being stifled, bridled and buried. What was Turtle Island like before all of this?

Fortunately for me I would learn about Turtle Island and the multitude of nations that lived on this land before the coming of the Europeans. The story is familiar to the ancestors of those who now live within European-created borders that artificially divided the continent of Africa and that continue to fuel the wars that we hear of today; it is a familiar story to those us from the Caribbean, Polynesia, India, New Zealand, Palestine and Australia. This is a familiar story to Greenland, Lapland and even Siberia. Yes, there are differences in our stories, but it is only by joining through our common experiences, searching in our past or — as the Twi word *sankofa* says — "going back and fetching it" that we can, perhaps, put a stop to this death project, once and for all. The Native American political prisoner Leonard Peltier recently wrote in *CounterPunch* about the horrific murder of Savannah LaFontaine-Greywind and the epidemic of violence against Native women, who are ten times more often victims of violence than any other group of women (the violence is enacted upon them by non-Indians):

> Whether America wants to believe it or not, the Native American people and their philosophy is crucial to survival of America. We have given our lives to protect the mother earth and bring to your attention [to] the destruction that this industrial society perpetrates against the natural ecology of this portion of the planet where we all dwell [...] It is time in history now that all the different religions, faiths and philosophies need to come together and actively, in a loud voice, seek change in America. Based on respect, for one another, the creator of all things, the mother earth and actively take part in bringing about this needed change of direction that America has taken for so long, for too long.[3]

Cunt-Tree: The Map to Liberation[1]

Son,

> O Great Grandmother Spirit give us your
> Peace so we can love as you love us
> Make us healthy so
> We can have a good life
> We praise you O Great Grandmother spirit

THE UNDISCOVERED COUNTRY, FROM WHOSE BOURN NO TRAVELLER RETURNS
— Hamlet

Country
Country
Country

What country are you from?

Country
Country
Country

What country are you from?

Country:
country |ˈkəntrē|
noun (pl. **countries**)

1   a nation with its own government, occupying a
    particular territory: *the country's increasingly precarious
    economic position.*
    • (**the country**) the people of a nation: *the whole
    country took to the streets.*
2   (often **the country**) districts and small settlements
    outside large towns, cities, or the capital: *the airfield is
    right out in the country | [as modifier] : a country lane.*
3   an area or region with regard to its physical features:
    a tract of wild country.
    • a region associated with a particular person,
    especially a writer, or with a particular work: *Steinbeck
    country includes the Monterey Peninsula.*

Middle English: from Old French *cuntree,* from medieval
Latin *contrata (terra)* **'(land) lying opposite,'** from Latin
contra **'against, opposite'.**[2]

Country
Country
Country

What country are you from?

Cunt
*
Tree

Cunt:
Noun
A woman's genitals

Middle English: of Germanic origin; related to Norwegian
and Swedish dialect *kunta,* and Middle Low German,
Middle Dutch, and Danish dialect *kunte.*[3]

Tree: tree |trē|
Noun

1 a woody perennial plant, typically having a single
stem or trunk growing to a considerable height and
bearing lateral branches at some distance from the
ground.
Compare with shrub[1].
• (in general use) any bush, shrub, or herbaceous
plant with a tall erect stem, e.g., a banana plant.
2 a wooden structure or part of a structure.
• *archaic or literary* the cross on which Jesus Christ
was crucified.
• *archaic* a gallows or gibbet.
3 a thing that has a branching structure resembling
that of a tree.
• (also **tree diagram**) a diagram with a structure
of branching connecting lines, representing different
processes and relationships.[4]

Cunt-tree.

What cunt-tree are you from?

What tree of cunts do you descend from?
What is your maternal lineage?
Who are the women who came before you,
what are the names that you cannot remember?
Or perhaps you do?
Stitch your lineage back together again.

Who is the woman through whose body you passed
between the unseen to the seen?
And who was the woman through which she passed?
And over and over again, all the way back

81

Until she is free.

And if you do not know -
how does that play into perpetuating the powers-that-be?
How does it play in strengthening patriarchy?
Why is it that the mother has been othered?
Why is it that the mother has been smothered?
Why is it that you know not your mothers?
Find out what gets in the way of that
knowledge.
And destroy it.

I think of the children torn from mothers.
I think of the children whose mothers were raped.
I think of the women whose lives are not valued.
Who are the women who came before you?
What are their stories?
What are their names?
Say their names.
Smash patriarchy with their names.

Cunt-trees have no borders.
Cunt-trees have no flags.
Cunt-trees have no military.
Cunt-trees have no visas.
Cunt-trees have no passports.
From cunt-trees we do not flee.

They are in y/our blood.

What is your cunt-tree?

—So, the next time someone asks you,

What cunt-tree are you from?

Start with the name of your mother. And your mother's mother. And if you should not know them, name the name of the woman/women who have mothered you. And if you are without that, invent them from the very fabric of mythology that have come before you, so that in your utterance they become real and present.

I believe it is in the answering of this question that paves the road to liberation.

I am the daughter of Beryl Balbirsingh
She is the daughter or Hildred Charles
& Hildred Charles is the daughter of
Frances Lopez who is the daughter of
Rose Lopez.

"THE UNDISCOVERED COUNTRY, FROM WHOSE BOURN
ALL TRAVELLERS RETURN"

In an attempt to do what those before could not do for me, I hope that by piecing our lineage back together again, through fact and conjecture, I can better equip you for life. I grew up with the knowledge that I shared the same birthday as my maternal great-grandmother, something that I was made to feel was of some import. Perhaps this explains why all my life, I have been obsessed with trying to decipher the whispers of the women in my family, with trying to salvage a story that would explain where I came from and how, perhaps, I could move forward.

The Forgotten Fathers

Son,

We must re-member our ancestors.

Who came before us? Why are we made to celebrate and commemorate the ancestors of our oppressors, but know not who came before us, our own heroes? Those who strove to free themselves from the shackles of slavery, the brunt of indentureship, the oppression of kings and queens.

Aside from losing our land, many of us have lost the system of knowledge that has existed even longer than this epoch that has been upon us in what is called modernity. This system of knowledge has been usurped by capital and profit, which have been and continue to be fuelled by the spoils of empire and the death project, including its ethnocide.

Where is your motherland?

What is the land of your mother?

What is my land?

I was born in Brooklyn. This occurrence equipped me with US citizenship. Any true student of American history must acknowledge the violent roots of this country. It does not take long to understand that the freedom that was heralded by our founding fathers did not include everyone, and has always been premised on our subjugation and theft. Even the US Constitution was inspired by the Iroquois or Haudenosaunee nation's Great Law of Peace.

When you were younger, you would often express embarrassment when we would go out and I would often stop to talk to others. "Do you know them?" you would ask, your brown eyes squinting at me, letting me know of your slight impatience.

Once when you were very young, you asked me, "Mommy, why do Black people smile at each other?" It was a fitting enough observation: whenever we took a walk and we came upon another Black person, a smile would often be exchanged. Intuitively, I knew the smiles were of recognition, not only of our presence here which, especially back then, was rare. But when you look into the annals of history — when you seek further than the textbooks and narratives insisted upon by the status quo — you learn a lot about your own history. You learn that your history has been buried so that another history could grow up from it, flower from it and, in the end, take all the credit (or sun, if we are to continue with this analogy). You learn to attach your own meaning to the blindfolded Moor's head.

One of my lifelong contemplations has been the connection/disconnection between me and my ancestry. Identity has always played an integral role in my life through the virtue of my skin colour. Identity politics, like intersectionality, seem to get some in a huff and a puff. Let me say a few words about this before I continue. In a *New Republic* article entitled "What Liberals Get Wrong About Identity Politics," Mychal Denzel Smith writes:

> Identity is the place to understand what forms of oppression are operating within your own life. From here, coalitions can be built with others who face similar forms of oppression, so long as it is also understood that oppression is not experienced the same across identities. This is where intersectionality, the theory developed by black feminist scholar Kimberlé Williams Crenshaw, is useful. It helps to understand that class oppression will look different for those who also exist at the intersection of marginalised race, gender, and sexual identities.[1]

He mentions the Columbia University professor Mark Lilla who wrote in a *New York Times* op-ed published ten days after the last election "that the age of identity liberalism must be brought to an end," because it has been "disastrous as a foundation for democratic politics in our ideological age." Smith continues,

> His main complaint is that identity politics is having a pernicious effect on the Democratic Party's ability to win votes from "the demos living between the coasts." He finds that focus on identity politics at the university level is to blame, since young people are not being taught that "they share a destiny with all their fellow citizens and have duties toward them."

But what Smith finds is that Lilla "spends very little time engaging the collective's meaning of the term, instead devoting his energy to his own interpretation of identity politics," which Smith reminds us was born in 1977 when a group of Black feminist scholars and activists called the Combahee River Collective wrote:

> We realize that the only people who care enough about us to work consistently for liberation is us […] This focusing on our own oppression is embodied in the concept of identity politics. We believe that the most profound and potentially the most radical politics come directly from our own identity, as opposed to working to end somebody else's oppression.[2]

However, when the Collective spoke about "our own identity" they were not speaking about their individual identities, but their collective one of being Black women: as they wrote, "If Black women were free, it would mean that everyone else would have to be free since our freedom would necessitate the destruction of all the systems of oppression."[3] Smith ends by asserting that the Democratic Party has co-opted this revolutionary language, and by doing so undermines this strategy.

In Trinidad and Tobago, race, class and social status are very much bound together — as witnessed recently in Anthony Bourdain's Trinidadian episode of *Parts Unknown*. The incident I'm alluding to is when the chairman of the Global Brands Group, Mario Sabga-Aboud (who has since apologised), bragged about the impact and success the Syrian Lebanese community in Trinidad has had despite its small size. The comment, seemingly devoid of many historical considerations, could even be viewed as being almost contemptuous to those of us who are the majority and descendants of enslaved Africans and indentured East Indians. It is true that race is a more malleable category in Trinidad and Tobago, but one would be remiss if one were not to acknowledge the seemingly large role it continues to play in terms of power and money.

I've always been fascinated by the way we choose to identify ourselves — intuiting early that of all the various ancestries I have coursing through me, it is as a Black woman that I identify. When I say Black, I mean those of us who have been scattered far from the African continent, representing through our skin a class of people whose exploitation was the very foundation and fuel of capitalism. When I say Black, I speak to our tenacity for survival and our spirit and the fact that our very existence assures us that our ancestors *are still here amongst us*. We are our ancestors. When I say Black woman, I acknowledge that for a greater part of our modern history, in fact, perhaps the very thing upon which modern history is premised, I was property, to be sold, abused without any repercussions to the white ruling class. This was the reality of my ancestors for this slither of time known as modernity. But I know that this brief history is not the only thing to inform my existence, but that if I were to go even further back, before the coming of Europe, there must have been women in my lineage who experienced a freedom that still alludes many of us today.

Identity politics does not mean that there is a magical bonding that takes place, necessarily, between people with common backgrounds. It does mean that there are areas of commonality that we can choose to galvanise ourselves around. In Trinidad, I would learn that anti-Blackness can be found among non-whites. Like the celebrated writer V.S. Naipaul, they have drunk the colonial Kool-Aid. They believe what they were taught by their colonial masters. So although I might exchange a knowing smile with others who look like me here in Denmark, let me be clear and say: it is not everyone who looks like you that will accept you. Again, you will know them by the work that they do. There is no homogenous movement for the liberation of the planet and its people.

* * *

Moving to Europe has only opened up my awareness of how far we as a people travel. It seems that wherever I travel in the world — from the Canary Islands to Southern Europe, from Sweden to Amsterdam — *we are there*. We are here, like others, for many various reasons but most importantly, if you look through the holes in history, you will learn that we have always been here. There. Everywhere. Human beings, no matter what ancestry, are usually more intrepid than we are led to believe. We often travel, migrate, in search of opportunity, novelty or even wisdom. Some of us are tickled by the energy of landing in a new place, forging new relations, and stepping on ground that has never before been stepped upon. Some of us have been uprooted and brought to places against our will. Some of us, to paraphrase Stuart Hall, just need to get away from our family.

But although we are everywhere, there is, I am afraid, a pervading, steady ignorance of our humanity as a people, which stems from a lack of understanding of history. Denmark, like so many other European nations who gained wealth through the plundering of the so-called New World and enslavement of Africans, devotes not much space in its school textbooks to the subject of slavery (as evidenced by my recent work with the theatre mentioned before), but much is devoted to World War II. To be fair, World War II is much more recent (most elderly Danes can still remember it) and Denmark had capitulated to the Germans during this period. While I can appreciate this fact, there is the point — made so eloquently by, again, La Vaughn Belle — that if more was taught about Denmark's foray into the business of plantations and enslaved Africans, there would be no by-now-cyclical news fodder of yet another "N-word scandal"; the most recent of which involved the tax-funded national radio station which hosted a programme for people to call in their most racist jokes. There would be a more nuanced understanding of migrations, wealth distribution and capitalism, even. Perhaps people would even begin to realise, on a greater scale, how the wars that have been waged in the so-called Middle East are also rooted in ideas of colonialism, capitalism and European/Western supremacy.

Denmark is a wealthy country and one of its most successful products is African aid. Yet no one realises that Europe extracts more wealth out of Africa than she sends in aid. But the practice of explaining to the populace how wealth is generated and moves around has never really been the business of schools and the state, anyway. I often wonder what education and the world would truly be like if we taught things like how the financial market really worked or other practical things such as how to fix a bike. Many of my students work in the banking industry and I sometimes ask, "Who owns the Danish National Bank?" To which many, incorrectly, will answer, "The Danish state."

Whether it's so-called progressive coloured folk from the Caribbean or even folks coming from Africa, the phrase "I'm not Black" says more about the person's lack of knowledge of their own history and the results of years of social conditioning to dehumanise and disempower us, than it does about their identity. The psychological and social consequences of this are certainly indicative of the level of discomfort many still feel around discussing race.

When human beings learn our history, the world will be a better place, to paraphrase the words of Dr Martin Luther King Jr.

You may not be familiar with the term "diaspora." It simply means "a dispersion of people from their original homeland." If you think about people of African descent, well, there were many reasons for us to travel the globe. Whether it was the glory of the intrepid and ambitious king of Mali, Mansa Abubakari II; or Maui from Egypt (or Persia, depending on the version of the story!) who sailed to New Zealand and populated Polynesia; or the age-old quest for land and food; or, lest we shall forget, that brutal practice of kidnapping and enslavement that so decimated and destabilised the population of Africa that some even say the continent is still recovering from it; or natural disasters, wars and terror, Black people have always had to be on the move. Check out stories of African historical presence and influence everywhere from Europe to as far as China. The best, in my and many others' humble opinion, is of course the work of Dr Ivan Van Sertima from Guyana.

I love the reflection of African diaspora, whether from the southern US, Caribbean, or South America, that held me in love when I was a child, growing up in Brooklyn. I do not love, however, the system that continues to impoverish and criminalise the poor and those who look like me. I do not love the seemingly state-sanctioned killing of my brothers and sisters. I do not love the prison system in the US that holds two million mostly Black, brown non-violent and poor people behind bars. I do not love the bigotry that fuelled the white settler mentality or the continued ignorance of how this system continues to this day. I do not love that in the US fifteen million children live below the poverty rate. I do not love the political system that only allows two very corporate-friendly political parties, who are really just wings of the same bird. I do not love that in 2016, the European Parliament reported that about ten thousand refugee children were missing in Europe, all fleeing a war that the corporate governments of the West have played no small role in instigating.

I am the child of immigrants. Your grandparents on my side travelled to the US like so many others, hoping to get what they felt they could not get in their native land: opportunity. You see, son, although Trinidad and Tobago was "blessed" with oil that has ensured a relatively stable economy, especially when compared to other Caribbean nations, there still exists a grinding poverty that could only be excused through the greed of capitalism. The Caribbean was not constructed to survive. It was never intended that former colonies would ever be able to truly compete with Europe and North America — to get a seat at the table. Even oil money cannot protect a people from the rotting system that was quite literally built to control, erase and dehumanise. *All of we is one, all of we is one.* But who *are* we? And who really is in control?

"One of the most disturbing consequences of colonization could well be this notion of a single History, and therefore of power, which has been imposed on others by the West," Édouard Glissant writes in his essay "The Known, the Uncertain." I often think about that time when I lived in Trinidad and how blessed I feel to have been there in the time I was. I got to Trinidad in the early Eighties and back then I felt that I was really given space to be a child. I was able to trade street fights for hopscotch, my unstable Brooklyn home for that of my grandparents. Sadly, violent crime now seems to be an all-too-frequent occurrence in Trinidad, with violence towards women topping the list. However, when I lived there, there was still a very strong sense of respect for our elders and each other. I'm no politician, but I often wonder how Trinidad and Tobago could be one of the wealthier Caribbean nations, but still roads, infrastructure, healthcare and education are not being prioritised. Ask any Trinidadian and they will say "Corruption." Unlike so many others, however, I do not believe that the governments in the Caribbean, Central and South America are any more corrupt than their European or American counterparts. History reveals that colonisation is indeed corrupt. In "Cross-Cultural Poetics" Glissant writes, "Many of us have never fully understood our historical times; we have simply experienced them. That is the case of Caribbean communities which only today have access to a collective memory."[5] It is true that Trinidad and Tobago has a rich culture, but this rich culture is despite its history of colonisation; and it is also true that there is something amiss in the land of my ancestors that longs to be righted, that longs to be balanced. "In one way or another, the Caribbean is the outgrowth of America," Glissant writes. "The part that breaks free of the continent and yet is linked to the whole."[6]

If you study the history of Trinidad and Tobago you will learn that it was always a country of bandits and excellence. Trinidad and Tobago is *bacchanal* — which, in local parlance, means "trouble" — good or bad. What can I tell you about the country of my parents' birth? That despite the excellence that she has produced and a flourishing if not minuscule upper class, there is grinding poverty and a violence that permeates the air. There is classism and racism, with some of their most blatant supporters being people who even look like you and me. I remember a few years ago, a Caribbean poet sat in my living room here in Copenhagen, a guest in my house, passionately defending the perceived difference between who she thought herself to be and African Americans. First of all, there have been so many migrations between North American and the Caribbean and throughout the Americas that we are all connected. Secondly, any Caribbean person who premises their superiority on that of the African American experience is clearly ignorant of the integral role this demographic has played in the liberation of Black people everywhere. It was indeed a sad, if not surprising day. Some of the greatest defenders of racism can sometimes be people of colour themselves. Internalised racism and misogyny are real.

In Trinidad and Tobago we are left with empty oil barrels, which we transform into an instrument — we being the descendants of enslaved Africans, we being the creators of culture no matter where we go, we taking the rhythm, the power of our beauty, we being the salt of the Earth. We who take the music of Europe and give it soul, we who inspire Picasso, we who are the labourers without which Europe could never have been built. It is the blood, sweat and tears of our ancestors that made the money for the large boulevards, docks and even government buildings here. If ever you go to Brussels, where the European parliament is headquartered, do not forget the ten million Africans who their King Leopold murdered. And still his statue stands.

In Trinidad, there is the beauty of Maracas Bay, of Blanchesseuse, of the food that reflects the African, the Carib, the East Indian. *All of we is one*, but all you have to do is read the comments to a local article that covers one of the all-too-frequent murders to understand the division that has often threatened and continues to threaten to tear the country apart, like the fault line that a beautiful

Trinidadian geologist once told me runs through Trinidad. Everybody knows that crime is rampant in the twin-island nation of Trinidad and Tobago — but like children in an abusive home, we do not talk publicly to outsiders about it.

I can also tell you that *God is a Trini*, a refrain uttered every year by Trinidadians as a testament to the fact that although these islands are in the hurricane belt, for some reason, we continue to elude them. Small countries always see themselves as big, and Trinidad is no different. Although we have a population of about 1.2 million, I am almost certain there is not a place on this planet a Trinidadian has not already been. From Trinidad and Tobago came Kwame Ture, the fierce writer behind the book *Black Power*, the late great C.L.R. James, the writing of V.S. Naipaul (whose own colonial confusion should not deter from the beauty and strength of his prose). We are the descendants of enslaved Africans, of indentured Indians, the conquered indigenous, intrepid Europeans and together we are stronger. Perhaps it may seem that we have lost our way in the shadow of empire, in the shadow of US neo-colonial policies, but there have always been those creating this path of freedom for us — we are not alone!

"What is the Caribbean, but a failed project of Europe?" a man in a rum shop once asked, somewhere in the middle of St. James, Trinidad. To everyone's surprise, he continued while pointing a determined finger into the air; the clink of the ice against the glass could be heard from the rum and coke in the other hand: "Europe is the opposite of Midas! Everything she does touch does turn to shit!"

Trevor Noah recently commented on the peculiar nature of colonisation, and I paraphrase here, saying that colonisation requires that the conquered people begin to act like their colonisers themselves. Some would say that I am as European as the next person and so who am I to criticise a system I have been so influenced by? But to this I answer:

I have survived despite this attack on my spirit, despite this erasure, despite this attempt to blind me from whence I came, despite this ethnocide! Part of the imperial project is to bastardise us, alienate us, cut us off from who we are. I cast off my blindfolds and so can see...

It is important that you understand, for example, that when slavery was abolished it was not, as the famous Dr Eric Williams once noted, due to the magnanimity of the European heart. It was because the enslavement of Africans was no longer deemed profitable. It is important that we comprehend that capitalism as we know it is built on slavery — whether we're speaking about hundreds of years ago or now. And tell me, why is it that it was the former slaveholders who were compensated for the emancipated enslaved humans and not the previously enslaved? What kind of insulting backwardness is that?!? And the descendants of these compensated slaveholders still sit atop the pyramid of power.

I find it ironic that it is often the same people who espouse the neoliberal idea of personal responsibility who tend to shun the idea of collective responsibility. As though human beings live in a vacuum. How can one claim that an individual is solely responsible for his or her life despite a system that created humanity based on the dehumanisation of the poor, Black and indigenous people the world over? Where is colonial responsibility? Why is it that Haiti, the first free Black republic of the so-called new world, was forced to illegally pay France billions for a war that liberated the descendants of enslaved Africans? Tell me, where is the justice in that? Why is the world not celebrating Haiti? Why is Europe, with her language of human rights and freedom, not teaching about this heroic feat that the once enslaved performed in order to achieve their liberation? A liberation that was inspired by the French, no less! Where are the statues in Europe to celebrate this?

Trinidad and Tobago. The southernmost of the chain of islands stretching from South America to North America. An archipelago of islands that was once home to the Arawak, the Caribs, the Taíno. Our history books tell us about the fierce Caribs from whom we get the word "Caribbean." Our history books tell us that they were cannibals. But is this true? Or is it a fabrication intended to justify annihilation?

* * *

Even when under the tyranny of my father and despite my youth, I understood his rage. If you are Black and you grow up in America, you do not have the "privilege" of not thinking about history and race. I say "privilege" because as far as I am concerned, it cannot truly be a privilege to get only a fraction of the story. From the lack of or very limited representation of Blacks in the media, to the very segregated housing arrangements that still overwhelming rules the day in the US, race was nothing I could claim I did not see.

However, let me pull forth the beauty that I experienced, the beauty that insists *despite*. There's the beauty of little brown girls, sitting between each other's knees as their hair is braided, much like when I braid your own hair. In this act we learn about the magic that is our hair, the beauty, the strength, the tenacity of spirit and of perseverance. When I braid your hair, I am taken back to Brooklyn and reminded of the beauty of brown girls jumping double-dutch, the jazz my father created in the living room, the comfort of sitting on my mother's lap, of hearing my sister spin yet another bedtime story for me, of my brother teaching me how to ride a bike.

Your grandfather is what happens to so many of us who are the descendants of a conquered people. As the great American writer and poet Langston Hughes once wrote:

"What happens to a dream deferred?"[7] As Hughes' poem goes on to wonder, your grandfather, Darlington Brown, exploded.

But before he did, this is his story. I share this story with you, son, only so that you can understand and appreciate the path that has been paved before you. Out of this darkness, your being can be rooted and fertilised. It is important that we remember both the stories of light and those of darkness, and understand that there are lessons to be gleaned from both. It is important that we do not forget these fallen fathers, the men who have come before us, as much as the women. May this story do him justice.

* * *

Darlington Brown, or "D.B." or "Chief," as he was affectionately called by his crew of friends, was originally from, as mentioned before, an area known derisively as "behind the bridge." This is an area in the capital of Trinidad, Port of Spain. "Behind the bridge" is a ghetto where the descendants of enslaved Africans paved their own way. And like all other areas dominated by Africans, it is a centre of cultural significance. I am writing these words not just for you son, but to everyone who is from this region and who may be reading my words now. Your grandmother, my mother, once took me there. In *Music from Behind the Bridge: Steelpan Aesthetics and Politics in Trinidad and Tobago*, author Sharon Dudley shares steelband historian Felix Blake's words on the socio-cultural concept of "behind the bridge":

> "Behind the bridge" is, geographically speaking, anywhere East of the Dry River which randomly provides a line of demarcation between the city of Port-of-Spain and its Eastern suburbs nestling jauntily on the hills of Laventille [...] The other meaning of "behind the bridge" is profoundly

sociological, providing clear reference to a person's socio-economic standing as poor, under-privileged and dispossessed—classic profile of the Afro-Trinidadian whose ex-slave forebears [sic] had settled in the hills of Laventille and who, three generations later, was still society's outcast...[8]

It is from behind the bridge that the youth engaged in stick-fighting or Calinda, a martial art, and Limbo — of which Sonjah Stanley Niaah writes in her book *Dancehall: From Slave Ship to Ghetto*:

The Limbo dance, for example, highlights the importance of not only the historical but also the spatial imagination. As a consequence of lack of space on slave ships, the slaves bent themselves like spiders. Incidentally, the lack of space in slave dungeons such as Elmina Castle, with characteristically low thresholds that the enslaved navigated to move from dungeon to holding room to the "door of no return" (now renamed the "door of return") before boarding the slavers is also obvious to the visitor. In the dance, consistent with certain African beliefs, the whole cycle of life is reflected. The dancers move under a pole that is consistently lowered from chest level and they emerge, as in the triumph of life over death as their heads clear the pole [...] The slaveships, like the plantation and the city, reveal(ed) particular spaces that produce(d) magical forms of entertainment and ritual.[9]

It is from behind the bridge that creative resistance was born, midwifing Trinidad and Tobago's world-renowned Carnival and steelpan, which was born out of the banning of drumming in 1884. Our drumming was banned because the British feared the coded messages being transferred through them; they feared that uprisings would be instigated. Our drumming that kept us close to Africa, that kept us close to the culture from which we came, was deemed illegal, like so many other aspects of our lives. It astounds me how much we as a people have been and continue to be policed, from our music to our hair to our movement. Has there ever been a group of people under more social control than Black people around the world?

Your grandfather, Darlington Brown, was born to Veronica and Joseph Brown, his father who originally hailed from St. Vincent. From what I was told by my father, his father was a carpenter and worked on the docks in Port of Spain. He also played the *cuatro* — a four-stringed guitar. I have had the privilege of meeting both my father's mother, Veronica Brown (aka Mommy Brown), and her mother, a slender East Indian and Carib woman who at the time was well into her nineties and lived in a beautiful wooden house in the village of Sangre Grande. I have heard, although I cannot confirm, that she was a feisty woman who owned her own house, and was married seven times, all to men of African descent. When I lived in Trinidad my aunt Bernice, my mother's sister, would take me to visit her, and I remember there was a picture of my father, your grandfather, in his youth, holding an electric guitar.

Your grandfather's appearance told a particular genetic story for those interested in the coming together of people. Remember, Trinidad is *callaloo*. Callaloo being the soup made from the large leaves of the cassava — a staple that, although it first made its appearance in the Americas, would spread to the people on the continent of Africa and all the way to the Pacific Islands. When we lived in Hawaii, the sight of the large leaves of the taro (what cassava is called there) filled my heart with a longing for Trinidad, my grandmother's cooking, and made me feel connected to the indigenous people of Hawaii.

One of the first things I discovered about my father was the beauty and elegance of his hands. His hands that told of his ability to fix, build and play the keys of his

Hammond organ. I would always see him in the faces and mannerisms of indigenous people the world over. I saw him in the Aborigines of Australia, some of the many diverse peoples on the continent we call Africa and when we lived in Hawaii, I saw him in the face of a Filipino man named Ray, who, like him, had had a stroke and was also once a keyboard player. At that time we lived in Paia, a small town in Maui where the locals were expected to depend on the dreams of tourists being cashed in on their island — not that much different than any other paradise tourist destination.

Your grandfather was part of a thriving music scene in Trinidad and Tobago around the Fifties and the Sixties, where local musicians created their own interpretations of jazz numbers and original pieces that harkened to the sounds of West Africa and Europe. He did this by the time he was sixteen — just a couple of years younger than you are now. He was an autodidact — everything he did and made followed what the sages over time have always said: the most efficient education is through doing, a fact which of course threatens the capitalist foundation of our education system.

Your grandfather, Darlington Brown, was what we call a *saga boy* in Trinidad, a well-dressed man who is usually associated with being "fancy" and many times a "ladies' man."

There are pictures of your grandfather in fancy striped suits, green velvet ones, and he was especially vain about his shoes. He often wore his hair in a high afro and his face was round, his moustache thin and straighter than the hair on his head. He played with some of Trinidad's biggest bands at the time including Clarence Curvan and Fitz Vaughan Bryan. He later made his own band, called Darlington and the Astronauts and, in fact, the only song that I have been able to find on the internet of his is from this band. It's a rendition of "Coming Home Baby" and you can hear your grandfather on the keyboard, along with other talented musicians. This time in Trinidad seems to have been a magical one. I was not yet born but your grandfather's music was a part of the cultural background to a post-war Trinidad and, to this day, it is not unusual to receive an email from someone who speaks his name with nostalgia. Someone once wrote this to me: "As I write this I am listening to an old Clarence Curvan CD on my computer and old Darlington Brown is revving away in the background. Funny, isn't it? He was good, too — the best. Pity he didn't go all the way to the very top."

Before he played the keyboards he taught himself how to play the guitar. His former bandmate, Puff, a man whom I'm in contact with and speak to regularly, tells me, "Your father had a talent — not only in music but in recognising other people's potential. It was your father who encouraged me to pick up the bass."

There's a picture of your grandfather in his band. It's an old black-and-white photo, and he can be seen sitting at his keyboard, his face full of India, Africa and the indigenous peoples of the area. He's surrounded by seven members, all beautiful and hopeful young men of the African diaspora — and his is the expression of perfection, of confidence, of love with the divine intervention of music which, evidently, transformed his life. This, my son, is your legacy.

Your grandfather left Trinidad with his first wife and child. His first son, Lerry, I saw last four years ago in 2013 during my most recent visit to the States. He looks like his father. Your grandfather was then married to another woman named June, a woman who acquired property throughout Brooklyn and Florida. No small feat for a woman from Behind the Bridge, Trinidad.

In Brooklyn, he found a job in Greenwich Village as an illustrator. Without formal training, that was quite an accomplishment. He lived at 147 Ocean Avenue, across from

Prospect Park in a beautiful two-bedroom apartment that would later be inhabited by the family he would sire with my mother. I remember that when I was a child, there was wall-to-wall carpeting and a telephone in every room — including the bathroom. In the living room of this Brooklyn apartment he had a Hammond B-3 and a Leslie speaker. There were hundreds of records. This living room became the go-to point for musicians from all over Trinidad and, as a child, musical jams were what filled my blood: from the congas to the bass, from the guitar to the tambourine. Son, I was nursed on the rhythms of the Caribbean, which championed Western music but, like Africans everywhere in the world, made it their own.

147 Ocean Avenue was the liming spot: to lime in Trinidad is to hang out, to chill, to drink rum and coke, to convene, to discuss life, religion and politics. Liming in Trinidad is an art; a societal and cultural invention and intervention necessary to digest the goings-on of one's life.

Most of the furniture in our living room was made by my father. There was the leopard-print couch and a wave chair. There was a large, circular, fifty-gallon fish tank which he designed and had made. Our living room was a shrine to jazz, with your grandfather having hundreds of records from Thelonious Monk to Pharaoh Sanders, from Miles Davis to Roy Ayers.

While I was attending college in Manhattan, I would sometimes go visit my father. By this time, he had arrived at a single-occupancy room in Brooklyn. One day I went to visit him and, as usual, I went through what was still then a very extensive record collection. Just earlier that day, your grandmother, my mother, had called me at work. "Lesley! Roy Ayers is playing at SOB's, let's go!" SOB's has always been one of New York's preeminent jazz clubs. I grew up with the music of Ayers and agreed to go with her. So that afternoon, while going through my father's albums, I found

the Roy Ayers Ubiquity album *Mystic Voyage*. I grabbed it —
"Can I take this? I'm going to see him tomorrow." After I left
I went to meet my friend in Washington Heights. We went
to a Dominican restaurant and who do you think walked
in? None other than Roy Ayers! I got my album signed and
I smile whenever I think of this story.

Your grandfather was a talented and beautiful man. My
memories of him include him cutting his own afro in the
bathroom mirror, the art that decorated our walls that he
painted while in art school, holding his hand as a little girl
through Prospect Park. I feared him the first many years of
my life — due to his capricious temper and tendency to strike
with belts. When he lost his temper, the entire family was on
lockdown, prisoners of his rage. Your grandmother would
often run away with us — but always unfailingly return.
There were times where the police had to be called, and he
was even once taken away for a psychiatric evaluation. I
have memories of late-night-through-the-window escapes,
fearing for our lives and the perpetual disappointment of
my mother always returning to him.

There was something about his rage that I always felt I
understood. Even at a young age I could see his frustration
— there seemed to be a disconnect between this man who
sat at his Hammond B-3 and played Kitchener's "Sugar
Bum Bum" — "*Audrey, where yuh get your sugah from?*"
— and the man who would sometimes, when work was
available, come home in the morning from a late-night shift
at the bank. He would always bring me a bag of peanuts
from work and when I was home sick he'd buy Jamaican
patties from the Junction in Flatbush for me as a treat. He'd
lost his job in the Village many years ago by then, although
our home was still full of the tools of his trade: drafting
boards, spinning pen-and-pencil holders, Letraset rub-off
letters that I would use to make my own, albeit childish
illustrations. Throughout the years living with my parents,

it was your grandmother who worked regularly while my dad's life was often punctuated by periods of joblessness. Once when I spoke to my mother about these things she confessed that she believed he never did recover from losing his job as an illustrator. "He was so talented," she said, not for the first time, and I was comforted by the obvious love my mother had for him.

Having to mother in another country myself has made me more compassionate towards my mother. There were many decisions made that I did not necessarily agree with, but I am learning to accept her for who she is, as opposed to what I wished her to be. Growing up in Brooklyn, I saw many independent, Black and doting mothers. Women who were fiercely protective of their children and ensured that they were enrolled in after-school programs, summer camps, even the Girl Scouts. Where my mother often came off as quiet and submissive in the shadow of my dominating father, there were other women who were anything but. Willie-Mae, my friend India's mother, was one such woman. She was independent, raising her children on her own, and had a stylishness about her that I longed to imitate when I grew up. I would spend every moment possible at Willie-Mae's and India's house, fascinated and soothed by their mother-daughter bond, their openness to me and the love of life that they both seemed to share. Willie-Mae and India never made me feel less than. My presence there was never questioned. Instead, I was made to feel warmly welcomed and included. I had some of my best childhood moments with them.

Willie-Mae and India lived on the first floor and their apartment, unlike my family's, was at the front of the building, which meant that they had a terrace, something I loved. Their front door was always left unlocked and I would visit *every day*. India was about a year older than me and I loved to hang around her. Willie-Mae would call me her girl. She would let me tag along wherever they went and even would buy me clothes when she took India shopping, something that my own parents rarely had the money to do. Willie-Mae owned a bar in Brooklyn but later became a nurse. I'll never forget helping her study for her nursing exam and how she passed it. She always talked about buying a house and some land down south. But I had lost contact with them years ago.

For many Trinidadians, licks are just part of life. For me however, I've often wondered about the relationship between licks and the enslavement and control of Africans and our bodies. I'm not saying that there were no cultures who did not practice physical violence against their children, but I would be remiss if I didn't say that even as a child, while I wept after a recent attack on my skin from leather belts, I would wonder how many in my bloodline have felt the sting of a belt or whip on their tender skin and desired a day when this will be no more.

* * *

My mother survived the days when we were young through work, and being that she was often the sole breadwinner, it was not unusual for her to hold two jobs. As a result, I was often home with my father. My father used to pick me up from the bus, and once when I got lost, he made a sign with my address to hang around my neck. There was a toy store right next to the DeKalb Avenue station where the school bus would drop me off, and sometimes we'd go in and he would buy me a little trinket. Once it was a plastic monkey that would flip around when I pressed the white buttons on the side. Sometimes he would give me drawing lessons or teach me something on the organ. Often, we'd lie side by side watching *Tom and Jerry* cartoons. I was always a loud child, but whenever I was around him I would lose my voice... until that day when he asked me why I was outside and my answer would lead to that hit on the side of my head. And now although he has been gone for so many years, whenever I get that ringing, I think about him without anger, but with a certain kind of sadness and wonder: "What really does happen to a dream deferred?"

* * *

Your grandfather, I must tell you, fell prey to crack cocaine in the Eighties and Nineties. There have been many narratives since then that suggest that the presence of this drug in Black and impoverished neighbourhoods was no accident, but that is beyond the scope of these letters. As the film *13th* and another entitled *The House I Live In* recount, "the war on drugs" is code for a war on Black and poor people. It is no coincidence that so many children of empire have succumbed to alcoholism, drug addiction and other forms of abuse. For some of us, there is no other way to cope with the violent system we have been born into, which insists on a shedding of our true selves and demands that we either align ourselves to capitalist systems and exploitation, or risk destruction.

By the time I was in college, my father had gotten clean but would soon be struck down with a stroke. His kidneys would fail him and he would have to become a ward of the State. In this home, he'd be able to have the dialysis treatment that he needed until he got another kidney. I wanted to help him — at one point he had even suggested that we live together. But there were a few instances I had experienced with him that let me know that he was still not in control of his temper, and there was no way I was going to willingly submit myself to his rage. As far as I was concerned, my days with that were over. It was a matter of survival.

He had also asked me to give him a kidney. But my father was still drinking alcohol and when I asked him if he ever drank water, he looked at me as though I had insulted him. I didn't want to risk giving him a kidney when he was still so obviously bent on self-destruction. It wasn't a difficult decision for me to make, but one that, I admit, I think about sometimes.

There's a picture of you in his arms that we took when we went to visit him during our New York stop on the way to Hawaii. He looks close to amused, and you're sporting this huge grin, and you're looking at him like you know this is a man you love.

It was not too long after we returned to Denmark that my mother called me to tell me he had passed away. She called because since I was the closest person to him, she wanted to know what I wanted to do with his body. Your grandfather had had a tantrum, stormed out of the home and some days later was found dead in the very Brooklyn streets he once walked through like a boss in his earlier years. A card that he had mailed to me some months earlier, arrived in Denmark. The card had been forwarded from Hawaii, and I wonder if perhaps he thought that I had never responded to it?

* * *

Life, I have found, if you pay attention, often sends you a life-saver when you feel you are drowning in the density of this world. One such life-saver for me was getting in touch with your grandfather's childhood friend, Puff. Throughout the few years that I have known him, speaking to him has helped bring me closer to my father, and in many ways, having Puff in my life has assisted in seeing the life of my father apart from my own. Through Puff and the wonders of Skype, I have learned that one of my father's greatest gifts was seeing the promise in others, and getting them to discover things about themselves that they had previously been unaware of. Somewhere along the way, my father became enveloped by the darkness that is perhaps a result of ancestors neglected for far too long, but I hope that through our lives, his life will be reinstated back into the light.

Knowing about our ancestors makes sense. Knowing about their lives can help us navigate our own, and it is my wish that some lessons can be gleaned from the stories that I share with you in these letters.

The Mothers of Memory: The Violence of Silence
(A Search for Womanhood, a Search for Truth)

Son,

Elephants, they say, rely on the wisdom of the matriarch — the grandmother — for survival. She remembers the watering holes, the droughts, the trees and directions. Etched in her memory is a map to survival based on the wealth of her experiences that could only have been attained through age. Studies have reported that older female elephants are wiser matriarchs and that they are better able to discern the difference between the presence of a threat or a friend. If this awareness is not there, the herd is more vulnerable. They also say that an elephant never forgets.

There are no elephants in Trinidad.

And my grandmother no longer has memory.

You have met your great-grandmother on a few occasions. A few times when I took you back to Brooklyn and Alzheimer's had not yet claimed her memory. Back then she was still her laughing and lively self, still dressing like the Queen of England, rolling her head back as a bubble of laughter gurgled through her being, reaching out from her gut and escaping her lips, and liking "to knock about" — so much so she still lived up to her nickname, "Hot Foot." When I was a child and lived with her in Diamond Vale in Trinidad, it was not unusual for her to awake before the rest of us, don her church dress and leather-buckled shoes, and walk to the Main Road where she'd either go to church or take the bus to San Juan (Sa-Wa) before the unforgiving sun of the tropics would belt out its heat. She'd go to the market and bring back okra so fresh that you could eat them raw, cassava, callaloo bush, tomatoes, *caraili*, mango, spring onions — her arms strong from garden work, her legs sturdy and beautiful. Do you remember when she visited us here in Copenhagen for her eighty-fifth birthday? Together with my mother, she travelled here to see us. You were only seven but you managed to take them into the centre of Copenhagen and back! I interviewed her about her childhood in an attempt to extract information about my family that I'd never before been able to, still trying to figure out if there is any connection between my great-grandmother and myself and the fact that we shared a birthday. I still watch this video, where she's laying on my bed, dressed in her slip, her hair fully grey, and I can see what I was unable or unwilling to see back then: her memory slipping away.

We took her to Tisvilde, to see Amigo, the summer house there, and she met the Danish side of your family. I'll never forget how she stood in the garden and in a complete old-school Caribbean common-sense kind of way said, "But there's room for another house here." Within a year your grandmother's aunt, Tanty Liv, a woman who has since passed, but who will always live in my heart, had built a house there.

Since I was not born on the shores of India, I was not given Kali to teach me the sacred act of destruction. Since I was not born in Africa, I was not given Yemeya the mother of the fish or Oshun. Instead, I was given a religion that taught me to continue to fear and revere the white man; I was supposed to believe that they too ruled in the spiritual world. I was taught that you did not upset God. And learned early not to upset my father.

Doh get god vex, he does see everything yuh does do!

Doh upset Daddy, he go give yuh licks!

But I was also given my grandmother, and when I am silent enough, I hear the whispers of Kali and Yemeya in her breath, despite her own forgetfulness.

My grandmother worshipped the great white man in heaven. She worshipped his mother too — although her religion forbids the worshipping of more than one god. And there is a spirit too, called the holy ghost, who she seemed to get along with quite well during her rendezvous with the Charismatic Movement in the Catholic Church. I think her body remembered Africa. When I would gently tease her about the colour of her god, she'd suck her teeth and say, "Chat man! Is only Americans who does talk about Black dis and white dat!" But we both knew that these legacies existed in Trinidad as well, although not as obviously, and that her own life had been impacted by them.

My grandmother had her altar, a dressing table overflowing with beauty offerings to Narcissus — creams that promised to remove the archipelago of brown spots on her otherwise pale hands (evidence of that which is not spoken but that which the body remembers), tweezers to pluck out the grey from her eyebrows until she barely had any left and left her eyelids droopy, lipstick tubes that bore deep holes in the centre (a testimony of this war-time child's inability to throw anything away) and nail polish which she would always call Cutex, no matter the brand. There was the giant white plastic bottle of talcum powder that she would dust all over her body with soft, large powder puffs, ostensibly to protect her from the seemingly tortuous heat in Trinidad, and generations of mothers would use this on their babies... a product that has now been proven to cause cancer. There were bottles of Limacol, Bay Rum, Canadian Healing Oil. The burning candles of saints for afflictions such as poverty and for protection. Her multitude of rosaries, some made of wooden beads, others of crystal and gold, and brightly coloured plastic ones, were draped over framed pictures and mirrors of different sizes, that ranged from Pope John Paul II to her dashing husband in his forties and an assemblage of grandchildren that ran the gamut of this family's ancestry.

There is so much that I do not know about my grandmother. Although I have asked her about my family, it always would seem as though she was reluctant to talk about something, as if she was hiding something. My "Ma," my grandmother's mother, is *creole* — the word my grandmother uses to describe people of African origin. Ma's husband is of East Indian descent. In Trinidad, when an East Indian and person of African descent have a baby, the baby is a *dugla*. Although my grandmother could pass for *dugla*, it has always been noted that she looks more southern European than anything.

There is the multi-coloured money of Trinidad and Tobago scattered across her dresser — the red one-dollar bill, green five-dollar bill and even the blue of the hundred-dollar bill — money so colourful, it looks fake. It lies there too, as if for the gods. There are statues — of a serene Mary, draped in white and blue; St Frances, my grandmother's favourite saint, and from whom the black Labrador that spent his life chained in the backyard would get his name: Gubbio; and of course Jesus, his eternally depressed and pained face seeing all that we did. When I was a young girl living with my grandmother in Diamond Vale, Diego Martin, it was not uncommon for my grandmother to impart what she had learned in life to me: *If yuh not careful you'll have all the boys lining up in front of the gate like dogs in heat.*

She was not always so unkind, but the threat of hosting a loose young girl in her house was enough for her to speak plain to me what others were, undoubtedly, saying about me.

It is not the location of watering holes my grandmother

has to pass on to me. It is not the journeys that I must transcribe into my heart, of places my grandmother travelled through in her youth. She cannot tell me where to go for a good price for fig at the market or where I can buy salt meat at a bargain. She can't tell me how to go to Moruga or why she thinks I should stay out of Laventille. She no longer remembers any of this. For me names like Couva, Manzanilla, Caroni and Todd's Road are towns I would look up on maps — never to be visited. "Dem coolie boys does only want one thing," my grandmother would warn me, seemingly oblivious to the fact that on my grandfather's birth certificate he himself was classified as a "coolie," a pejorative term for East Indians that caused him some pain. In my family, words and phrases like coolie, creole, niggah, chinee, white man, "she feel she white" along with all their possible fusions such as "niggah chinee," "coolie niggah," and "white niggah" are all used with impunity. This irreverence for race, like that of so many other Trinidadians, seems to stem from the idea that since we are a mixture of all, then we have a right to ridicule each of them equally. But in my family's mixture I am taught through jokes they have inherited and attempted to hand down to me that we are privileged because we are mixed. I do not like these jokes. I do not like it that growing up, I would be chastised for having darker skin or kinkier hair, nor that the mark of beauty is how white — or in Trinidad, how *Spanish* — you look. In America I felt beautiful, in Trinidad I was sometimes made to feel by some in my own family that I was too dark. I was raised in Brooklyn and I had learned that Black is beautiful through the love that enveloped me while in the presence of my friend India and her mother Willie-Mae. Although colourism has been and continues to be a challenge in Trinidad and many other places around the globe where there are communities of colour, I was able to meet others whose minds had not been infected by this legacy of colonisation, but rather were empowered by the motto "Black is Beautiful!" My experience and education in Trinidad made me realise how much more brutal (if such a thing could even be possible) the institution of slavery was practiced in what is now the United States as compared to many of the countries in the Caribbean, with some exceptions, of course. My fourth-grade teacher in Brooklyn had encouraged her students to think about the Native Americans. And it was in Trinidad that I learned about the Arawaks and the Caribs, the East Indians, the Africans, the Syrians, the Lebanese, the French, etc., who all came to a small island, off the coast of South America.

* * *

Although we are a nation known for our ritual of national bacchanal called "Carnival" — where the pressures of politics and social issues are vented in a somewhat controlled manner — there have always been distinctions cast as far as what being a "good" girl or woman was.

Yuh fas', eh?
Yuh rude, eh?
Yuh loud, eh?
Close yuh legs, nah!

In Trinidad and Tobago there is a prominent culture of catcalling called "suiting." Depending where you are in Trinidad, no women (sometimes even young girls, for that matter), are safe from this. When you *suit* a girl or a woman, you are talking her up, trying to get an in. Part of *suiting* involves a *psss...* Sometimes the remarks are funny, truly reflective of the inventive nature of Trinidadian culture. "Peanuts," a man once called out to my teenaged cousin, "Why yuh skin so red?" Other times, the attention is more cutting — "Yuh dry, eh?" (dry is a derogatory word for thin) — but either way as a woman you have to learn to not let it get under your skin. *It just is.* In *Moving Beyond Boundaries: International Dimensions to Black Women Writing*, Carole Boyce-Davis writes:

> [S]exism, its manifestation, the perception of women, is not very different in the US than it is in the Caribbean. Perhaps the only difference is that, in the islands, men mask their sexual exploitation of women in the social area of entertainment, namely dance which traditionally has been an avenue for courtship. Consequently, women appear openly to welcome their defilement as prize. Women trying to buy homes on their own or obtain passports for their children are faced with a demand for a man's signature, a man's presence[1]

On a worn-from-age, fragile, off-white paper, there is a letter that I still keep. It was written to me when I was eleven by my grandfather, and although it never made it to me during his lifetime, it was found in his Bible after his death and, thankfully, shared with me. It reads:

February 1, 1985

My Dear Lesley-Ann — you are not <u>even</u> in your <u>teens</u>. I have spoken to you on <u>many occasions</u> about the following:

1. Giving the salutation of the day i.e. good morning etc.
2. Staying for a long period of time on the phone and constantly speaking of things of no or little importance.
3. Your loud talking and laughter.

4. Chatting with the boys in front of the gate or in the garage on occasions.
5. Taking frequent walks out of the house, sometimes without permission.
6. Going to the "mall" on regular occasions.

If you would not like to be embarrassed in the future, please curb the above practices as these are not becoming of a little girl. No comparison should be made between yourself and the others, as they are considered adults and you a mere little girl.

My poor grandfather. Old-school gentleman having to take care of a bubble-gum-chewing, neck-switching, Brooklyn girl. It's hysterical when I look back at it, understanding what I do now. My grandfather genuinely loved me, he just couldn't stand the little American girl that I was.

Words most often used to describe me when I was growing up were "fast" and "fresh." "Fast" was usually said without the "t" as Trinidadians have a way of being more economical with time where words are concerned, and "fresh" had not yet come to be infused with the positivity it would later be associated with in the late Eighties and early Nineties through African American culture. To be "fresh" is to be too inquisitive, too sassy, too smart even, in some cases. Our legends are rife with gender-based bias as well. Soucouyant is a blood-sucking witch who sheds her skin. La Diablesse is the female devil, who seduces men with her charm and hides her calf foot under her dress. Sparrow the Calypsonian sings, "Sell the Pussy and bring home all the cash to me." A woman who is "gone tru" (through) is without hope; usually because she has slept with too many men. Christine was your grandmother's cousin who I would sometimes see in town liming in rum shops and drunk, and who would eventually contract HIV and die of

AIDS. When I look back at her, I just want to ask *who did this to you?* I wonder, as her behaviour I now know could be related to early childhood sexual abuse. "Young ladies should be seen and not heard," my grandfather would often say to me, a righteous finger pointing in the air. *A "bat" is a loose woman…*

I was fas' when I was growing up because I experienced my childhood as something to get away from. Too young to go to school, I would often begin my day, holed up in the bedroom I shared with my brother Gerry and sister Shelley-Ann in Brooklyn (who were both in school), by watching *The Magic Garden*. I loved this show — two hippie women who played the guitar replete with talking squirrels and chuckling flowers. After this program, I'd watch an array of black-and-white television shows such as *The Munsters* and *The Addams Family* — shows that allowed me some comfort that my West Indian family was not the only strange one in existence. My mother would typically be at work, and my father napping, playing the organ or on a trip to the local store. I'd very often read and write stories using my mother's manual typewriter. Every summer while my friends went down south to reconnect with family, my brother, sister and myself would stay at home. Although most of our family was in Trinidad, my brother and sister only returned to Trinidad after becoming adults.

* * *

A bat! A bat! A bat! It was an entire car filled with teenagers. We had just gotten home from Midnight Mass, so it was Christmas. I lived with my grandparents in a grey concrete house on Emerald Drive. This house was one of the first houses built in our neighbourhood and I remember my grandfather always telling us that it was built for Dr Eric Williams' daughter. We lived in a valley in a neighbourhood called Diamond Vale, in Diego Martin. Diego is pronounced *Diggo*. Every street in Diamond Vale is named after a precious gem. It was a car full of girls that I had not known. It was probably a year since I had moved to Trinidad from Brooklyn. I had never been with a boy. But still, the girls yelled, out into the midnight street, "Bat, yuh ole ting!" I felt ashamed. I felt lonely. I felt out of place. Instead of making me feel even more ashamed of the incident, my grandmother protected me. First, she cursed the car off, in the way only Mummy Hildred could do, wielding words like "cunts" and "asses" like a cutlass to cut the hatred down that filled the air. Then she looked at me, with no suspicion or judgment and in a silence that was healing, hugged me, and we walked back into the house together. I was only eleven.

No matter where I travelled within the realm of my family, Catholic icons would follow me — hanging from walls, adorning candles, calendars and other décor around the house. There was the Jesus in perpetual pain, on the cross; or the Jesus with the burning heart; St Francis statues and a depiction of the last supper. Mary, Jesus' mother played a special role in our home, as with most Catholics, and I could never wrap my mind around the idea that God *told* her she was going to have his baby rather than *asked* her. When I asked my grandmother about this, she would laugh and suck her teeth, incredulous at the audacity I always seemed to have on display as a child. "Eh-eh," she'd say, "You fas' eh? You better be careful with that fresh mouth of yours!"

I was called "fas'" my entire life. "She too fas'!" is a refrain, pregnant with disdain, that shoots out of the mouths of women instead of loving girls, instead of nurturing us, teaching us. These refrains become a noose that is thrown at the first sign of a girl's intellect, that tightens itself around her neck the older she grows. If she learns not to silence herself, the women around her will. This is what being complicit in patriarchy demands.

* * *

My grandmother visited us often in Brooklyn when I was younger and before I moved in with her in Trinidad. And when she visited, I felt a certain calm around me. Our usually chaotic home seemed to fall under her maternal and orderly spell. I loved hugging her and smelling her dinner-mint-tinged breath and watching her take her dentures out at night. She would put them to soak in a bowl and then make faces with her now sunken mouth. "Ah sexy, eh?" She'd tease, laughing and hugging me. But there was something else about Mummy Hildred that always jumped out at me. It was not something the family talked about often, but it had to do with her skin colour and how incredibly light she is. It also had to do with the archipelago of spots on her hands and up her arms, the ones she would rub hydroquinone-filled cream on every evening, hoping that they would disappear.

> As the first and oldest mother, the matriarch is instrumental in teaching her daughters how to care for their own young. Once they start to bear babies, their sisters will assist in childcare. This provides training for them, preparing them for their own first calves. Elephant mothers are attentive to the needs of their young. Babies are born with almost no instinctive patterns, nearly everything they do has been taught to them by their mothers and aunts. What they get taught will vary according to the matriarch and her herd[;] different groups face different dangers and bear different responsibilities. The matriarch will determine what is important for that specific herd and mothers teach the young ones accordingly.[2]

My mother is a bastion of secrets. Her fortitude in the face of my questioning is magnificent. I ask her questions so that I can learn. What is it to be a woman? What does it mean? Why must women always "wait for men," as I am often told? My mother sucks her teeth and blows me off like an annoying insect hovering in her space. She will not tell me that my brother has a father different than mine. And, if it were not for pictures, she would not even have told the true colour of her hair. I do understand she is of another time — but I have often wished that she would see that so am I, and so in that spirit, share with me her life experiences.

"Shhh." She would say, alive with a glee that should only be reserved for the adolescent, "Don't let Mummy Hildred (her mother) hear us. She does get vex when she feel we bad talking Ma."

* * *

It is February when I travel to Trinidad for the first time with you and your father — in other words it is the first time I have travelled to Trinidad as a woman. We visit Trinidad not too long after we returned from Maui. The trip is a lesson in how difficult it is to sleep in the home of my youth. Every wall and every crevice reflects a magnified dream inebriated by youth, torn asunder by age. One day, in an attempt to reconcile the past with my present, in a gesture borne out of the homage I yearn to pay to my youth, I walk out to the backyard of my grandparent's house to smoke a cigarette behind your back. I had been successful in quitting during my pregnancy with you, and while I nursed you, but it did not take long for this habit to take hold of me again once you were weaned. I don't want you to see me smoke because I attempt to protect you from this dreadful habit I still struggle with. It is a typical blistering hot Caribbean day where the sun nails everything down with its steely glare, and my eyes rest on the same hut-spotted hills my eyes rested on as a child, when my mother, her own keeper of secrets with newly dyed auburn hair and freshly painted orange toenails, shuffles up to me and says, "Ask Aunty Glenda, she will tell you everything." For one moment it appears my usually erratic mother is present.

So my mother organises the visit from Diego Martin to Santa Cruz to visit Aunty Glenda. You may not remember this trip, so long it has been now. Without a car, we rely on my eighty-year-old Uncle John and the same powder-blue car he used to drive my cousins and me to Maracas Beach in our youth. The gentle breeze prods memories of brown limbs next to other brown limbs and red nail-polished chipped nails holding onto plastic door-knobs and the smell of sweat and salt mixed with the excitement of getting closer and closer to the sea, as we pant and our hearts beat wildly, like a lover finally allowed to see her beloved, driving through the lush landscape that takes us there. There would have been a pot of *pelau* in the trunk, with a cooler of Carib beer, cola and a bottle of rum. On the way, my uncle would pull over to buy fresh coconuts and, if we were lucky, mangos. To get to Maracas from Diego Martin we would have to drive through the rainforest and pass numerous springs that fall out of the side of the mountains, impregnating the air with a freshness and vibrancy that only spring water can bestow.

My mother, her own keeper of secrets and perhaps relieved to redirect my prodding into her past onto someone else, comes as well, along with your father (disoriented by the general disorder of my family and by extension Trinidadian culture) and you, whose hearing impairment serves you well amidst the squawking of my family. The road to Santa Cruz winds through the lush and wet grasshopper-green hills. Despite his eighty years coupled with his third pre-noon beer, my Uncle John handles the road expertly. I watch you as your little eyes fall on the same wild, lush green hills that we must drive through, and I feel as though I am experiencing a miracle: to bear witness to you taking in the very same land my ancestors had once tread (how blessed am I?). I know the route well, and I hope that one day you can say the same.

We pull up to the house where my great-grandmother, Frances Lopez, died in Santa Cruz, not too far away from the cemetery where she is buried. "Crazy" Aunty Glenda lives there now. This house holds many secrets that I did not know at that time. Like the loves that were not allowed, the babies not born, and why the garden had been tended with such care.

As I enter the leaning, wooden house, I notice the copy of James Joyce's *A Portrait of the Artist as a Young Man* that props up an uneven bookcase. The house is wooden and leans. It stands on stilts and the beaded curtain between the living room and kitchen is made of bright, yellow plastic. It is the type of house I would want to own and live in. We sit in the kitchen where Aunty Glenda serves us sorrel from old soda-drink bottles and complains, "The fridge not working, and I have no money to buy ice." In the Caribbean, ice is a luxury among the poor. I notice that one of her eyes is cataract-coated. I also see she lacks vanity and has a towering conviction to be herself. Instinctively I just feel love for her. When my mother demands, "Tell Lesley what you was telling me the other day, nah," she replies, "I don't know what there is to talk about. You can't start up a story like that."

"But tell me…" I urge.

"I don't know where to start myself," she insists. We are all sitting around the kitchen table that is covered by a plastic, flowered table cloth.

"Start with where Balbirsingh (my grandmother's husband) used to challenge Hildred on being the white man child," Uncle John offers. "You the white man child!"

My grandfather would shout, in a bout of drunkenness. My grandmother would sing about the sufferings of Jesus to drown out his voice because my grandfather was her cross to bear. We sit laughing at the memory of my now long-dead grandfather and his insistent prodding at my grandmother's parentage, but Aunty Glenda catches herself. "I'm not going to sit here and laugh at my mother, you hear?" We assure her that is not our intention. I am afraid we have insulted her, and her face, which was once open and willing, shuts down. I panic. Has she changed her mind? But she adds, "Oh wait, let me show all of you this." She gets up and walks to the other room and begins to rummage through an old photo album. Her hair is cut short, her face broad and she has an angular jaw. She is a sun-roasted brown and wears a flower-splashed housedress.

"You see sometimes I does see things but I don't remember where I see them, but I have a few pictures I want all you to see." She hands us a picture, "You know anybody that look like this?" And, as a matter of fact, we do. He is the spitting image of my grandmother's youngest son, Darius. My Uncle John, the self-appointed racial expert, exclaims, "He have white in him, you see how light he is? See the structure of the nose and thing? That is French. Don't mind he head curly." I give him an exhausted look. "But who is that man?" I ask. I have seen this picture before. I found it once, in one of my childish archaeological digs throughout my grandmother's things. Everyone in my family knows that as a child, I liked to dig. I would dig into the brown or black leather purses of my mother. Zipping or unclasping the purse open, I would dip my slim brown hand into the velvety softness of the purse, almost dizzy with reverie. Out would come compact powders as brown as tamarind, lipsticks the colour of dew-kissed roses and sometimes, much to my mother's embarrassment, birth-control devices. If I were lucky, dinner mints and pens would be transferred from her possession into mine. There was certainly a period in my life where nothing was more exciting to me than my mother's purse. Hands down. One day I chose the space under my grandmother's bed as my Treasure Island. I dug into suitcases speckled with the dried-out shells of insects, and among a wooden crucifix of the eternally suffering Jesus, old bottles of half-used Limacol and Bay Rum. There was a bottle of holy water in a plastic bottle and a soft candle wrapped up in brown waxy paper. Among these things I had found a picture of this man my Aunty Glenda is now showing us. "Who is this man, Mummy Hildred?" I had asked. "Is this Pa?" Thinking it was my great-grandmother's husband. My grandmother had sucked her teeth, unwilling to part with anything she might have known, "You like to dig, eh?" And she dismissed me with a sly look in her eyes. "Who is this man?" I ask Aunty Glenda, and I continue, "Because Mummy Hildred has a picture of him."

"He must be your great-grandfather," Uncle John suggests. "See, hear the romance here," and Uncle John begins to read the message on the back of the picture: "1924. Let happy memories spring to life again and may it's *something something*... I can't make out the handwriting there... thoughts surround us all." Aunty Glenda assures us, "I don't have no whole story, just pieces." But it is the pieces I need. I want to tell Aunty Glenda that all of us who are borne of my great-grandmother hold a piece of her story, and together, we can make her dreams whole again. But instead, like my grandmother and mother, I remain silent.

It is not until years after this episode that I am able to understand the true magnitude of this story and its importance in my life. It is not until I am in my forties that I understand what this longing inside of me has been — what I have been looking for in this story. There is something about the story that now that I am older... I can appreciate that it is not the Mills & Boon-type romance between my great-grandmother and this man, in the way it has been suggested by family members in low whispers and chuckles as if this could ever be a romance of equals.

It could not have been a romance. He owned the cocoa plantation. My great-grandmother and her husband were his employees. That would be like calling Sallie Hemings Thomas Jefferson's girlfriend. I am lucky enough to have a picture of my great-grandmother and her husband, and the way that they stand together is telling. He is eager, stepping forward while she holds back, her face etched in deep sadness. How many generations of sadness is she wearing on her face? Is this the sadness that I too have felt, throughout my life, especially when violations against me have been brushed aside, as so many women are taught to endure?

It is not unusual for a child to want to know the stories of those who came before her. There was a time, no matter where in our lineage you go back to, when those that came before us understood the importance of maintaining the stories of our ancestors and so handed them down, keeping them intact and so alive in our very breaths.

* * *

I understand now how people lose it all.

It was a sunny autumn day and it was recess. I was in the fifth grade and playing double-dutch with my usual crew of Caribbean and African American friends. There was Tracy — her colourful beads creating music as she jumped the pop-up or turned the ropes. There was Monifa — also from Trinidad — and of course, the twins Andrea and Deidre. Double-dutch was one of my favourite games to play. It didn't cost anything and all you needed was a decent rope and at least two other girls who weren't double-handed. The best rope to be had was telephone wire, and I had become an expert at spotting Bell telephone vans and running them down to secure some. It was typical Brooklyn spring weather that day: warm sun beating down through the leaves of the tree-lined Midwood Avenue casting lacy shadows onto the pavement. We were hot and Monifa and I were thirsty and had decided to go inside, to the gym, to get some water from the fountain. I can still remember to this day how we relished the cold water that sputtered out of this shiny, porcelain fountain. We weren't supposed to go inside unattended. But we were kids, and we were thirsty.

P.S. 152 was the last school that I would attend before being sent to Trinidad to live. I had entered the school in the second grade, at the very end of white flight — that time when all the white people in my area in Brooklyn were leaving to move to bigger and better things in Long Island, New Jersey and other suburbs where there was more space and, more importantly, that were devoid of people of colour. Their exodus meant that African American families and other families from the African diaspora could find beautiful apartments with affordable rents, and my family was one of them. Flatbush back in those days was buzzing with salsa, calypso, reggae, soul music. It was right before Reagan and promise was ripe. My African American friends were always dressed to the nines with freshly greased faces that told of attentive parents, and they bore names of Black revolutionaries like Jomo Kenyatta.

That year was the second year I had been in an IGC class, which stood for "intelligent, gifted children," but aside from things going completely wrong at home with my father and his rages, something else was about to go wrong for me.

The gym, empty, was huge to both of us, as our little bodies stood in the vastness of the room. But we knew we'd be fast and soon return to our double-dutch. I loved the gym and its shiny wooden floors and how it made our sneakers squeak. Everything seemed to happen so fast and

I'm not sure the sequence of events — but it involves a group of boys, all shorter than Monifa and myself, which told me they were younger than us. That was the first thing I noticed. However, it didn't take Monifa and me long to realise that we were in danger.

Some of the boys held Monifa back. The others pinned me to the ground. There was a boy holding each of my arms down on either side above my head and two others at either leg. I fought and tried to pull free but to no avail.

I was struggling.

I was scared.

I was pinned down and my pants were being pulled off. As my clothes were being peeled off there was one boy who, through what he said, made me realise, even back then, that he had seen someone do this to someone else. My second thought went to the woman he had witnessed it being done to. My third thought went to all the women who had ever experienced this. It was awful to be held down against my will, to feel my clothes being pulled off... to hear what these boys were saying as they laughed and taunted me. This was a violent sexualisation that immediately gave me access into the portal of terror that too many suffer at the hands of others.

Miraculously, my gym teacher walked in, just in the nick of time. Mr Shark was a tall, thin, dark-haired man who wore glasses. He seemed shocked and reacted quickly — demanding everyone to leave the gym. He spoke to Monifa and myself, reacting as though whatever had gone down was our fault because we should not have been there. He told us to go back out to the playground.

I went home that day and told my mother. She was organising the laundry. My mother worked two jobs at the time and was usually very tired, when I did see her.

"Mummy. Something happen to me today." I always spoke to my parents with my Trinidadian accent.

"What's that, Lesley?" My mother was focused on the laundry.

"I was attacked in school."

"Attacked. Like how?"

"A group of boys held me down and tried to take my clothes off –"

"Lesley, you have to forget about it. And don't tell your father. You know how he does get."

And that was it.

It wasn't too long after that that I was sent to Trinidad to live with my grandparents. The reason was that I was "too American" and my behaviour took a turn for the worse right before being sent away. I hadn't made the connection before — but I do remember thinking, at the age of ten, that if I didn't leave Ocean Avenue, jail and pregnancy were options. This is not to say that every young Black girl in my neighbourhood felt this way. There were no shortage of families and parents who ensured that their children stayed out of trouble. Many of the other children I grew up with did well in school and avoided fights. The issue with me was that I had no one, except my father and his very corporal discipline which eventually became less and less effective the older I got, to ensure that I stayed out of trouble. I stopped going to school shortly after this attack. Back then, however, I had not made the connection that this avoidance of school was connected to a diminished sense of safety there. Instead of going to school I would wander the streets of Brooklyn, alone, walking all the way to Avenue H, sometimes from the Junction to Hudde High School. These walks exposed to me the very segregated nature of Brooklyn, where I would walk from one block to the next, and find, like Narnia, worlds that were different than the one I had grown up in. The character of the neighbourhoods would change — whether it was a Jewish neighbourhood or Italian — and I often have wondered how did I appear, a young girl, walking these streets during school hours?

When I did go to school I started hanging out with the kids in Ms Horowitz's class, which was considered the worse class in our grade, but I liked the kids. There was Poochie, who was the handball king, and Makeba who I knew because my mother would always let the Jehovah's Witnesses in the apartment when my father wasn't home, and they happened to be Makeba's mother and sister. I began to fight more and had asked my mother to take me out of the IGC class because, get this, I thought it was too elitist. While that was not the word I used, I explained that I didn't want to be in a class that was considered better than other classes, because I believed we were all the same. My mother, too exhausted to argue with me, went along with the my plan, and after having a long talk with my principal, Dr Shapiro, agreed to the change. At around that time I'd started to smoke in the bathroom, so much so that my principal decided to kindly ask me to step outside whenever I had wanted to smoke. Again, I was only in the fifth grade. By this time, I didn't even consider the incident in the gym. Everyone I had told — the gym teacher who had walked in on the assault, even my mother — did nothing. I suppose I swept the incident aside to cope with the harsh realisation of that message. I was eventually kicked out of the school when it was discovered that I had a razor blade on me. I had decided to take it to school one day because I had heard through the grapevine that I was going to get jumped.

I became very destructive. I was "boy crazy." And it was this version of myself that landed in Trinidad amidst my Catholic family.

It wasn't until I was in my late thirties that these memories returned to me. I didn't remember this until I began feeling intense social anxiety. Looking back, I can see how it all started to unravel for me — a culmination of a change of job, yet another move, the loss of a baby and learning about your uncle, my brother's, imprisonment. I had accepted a new job and with that was required to give up the beautiful apartment in Oesterbro that had become our home. In a rush to find a place to live, I bought an apartment which we moved into. It was a great location, as it was not too far from your father. However, I was to later learn that it is very often life-altering events such as moving that trigger early childhood trauma: moving and changing jobs.

I asked my mother about the incident in gym, but she could not remember the details, although she did say it rang a bell.

My question was, why didn't she do anything about it? But I knew one of the reasons. My mother was overworked, mothering three children in a foreign country, and had an overbearing and violent husband. But it didn't make the pain any less. Why didn't my mother do anything? And then I think about my great-grandmother. No one tells you her story. It's locked into people's hearts and their lips are shut. Whenever I do try to get the story, the response always has something to do with sullying her name. But, if there were transgressions, which seems to be the likely case, then why are we protecting that story and relating it to besmirching her name? Why is it always the women and the men who are violated that are left to feel the shame? The hurt? The guilt? Why does this system seem to protect the perpetrators?

My Aunty Glenda told me on that day we visited her in Santa Cruz that the owner of the plantation would sometimes call my great-grandmother and make her walk for him on the gallery. He would have his nephew — a child left behind by his Corsican father (who was the brother of the man who owned the estate) who had impregnated one of the East Indian workers in the barracks — sit by his side. This nephew is the man in the photograph. My Aunty Glenda told me that this little boy would be taken out to the barracks to visit his mother, but that he lived in the house with his uncle. This little boy, about the same age as my great-grandmother and her husband, was her husband's cousin. I have not seen too many pictures of my great-grandmother and, in all but one, barely can recognise even a smile.

There was always a family that my grandmother engaged with. They had long left Trinidad and had settled in Queens by the time I knew anything about them. The whispers would say how much my grandmother looked like them. That they were the legitimate children of this man. This could mean that they were my grandmother's half-sisters. No one ever acknowledged this out loud. I wonder if this ever had anything to do with the great sadness my grandmother would sometimes express. Sometimes she'd say to me in Trinidad, "I know how it is not to be with your mother" — as she did not live with her parents, but was raised by another woman, her *Nennen*.

* * *

If you walk from Diamond Vale to the Main Road and go via Sandale Road, you will see colourful flags hoisted in the air to signal the presence of Hindus. For Diwali, the many streets and villages are alight and India's rich culinary tradition has become part of Trinidadian heritage as well, as can be seen with some of our national dishes, *roti*, *pholourie*, doubles. One of the major gods in the Hindu pantheon is Ganesh, the remover of obstacles. When I search my lineage in an effort to build a roadmap for you, son, I know that part of our East Indian heritage is from a Sikh — but I am unsure of how he arrived in Trinidad. Just as Africa is coursing through our veins, so is India — whether it is through the name Baboolal or Balbirsingh or the countless others that we will never know. It is important to remember that despite what seem to be great grievances between the two groups in Trinidad, there are many of us who are living testimonies to a comradery between the two, borne out of necessity.

I realise that this is how it works for many of us women. *How the silence is handed down.* That there are many girls, like myself, who go to someone and tell of a sexual transgression, and the adult tells them, "Hush up, nah! Don't tell nobody!" Thereby giving the shame to the victim and giving the perpetrators further license to violate. This project of modernity depends on this. From profiting from the rape of our ancestors to upholding the capitalist patriarchal system under which we live — this system favours and even protects sexual predators. This is how it works. When we look back at the history of slavery, of indentured labourers, tell me, who could a child go to tell of a violation? A woman? A man? Who was there to protect you? How could you protect yourself from the plantation owner? The overseer? Even family members? Tell me, how many generations of rape has colonialism sanctioned? Rape is a colonial tool. *Keep silent* — this is how many have protected their children. Themselves. But this silence is violence.

* * *

On my last trip to Brooklyn, my mother and I visited her youngest sister, Aunty Majorie. Aunty Majorie is the youngest girl of my grandmother's three daughters and she is my grandmother's caretaker. She is the owner of various properties throughout Brooklyn, something she admonishes my mother about. "Look at how many years you live here and you still doh have nothing," she says, forgetting about the pampered life that her marriage of convenience has granted her with.

My grandmother, with her social-security checks deposited in Brooklyn, has no memory. Her body is strong — it reflects her life of eating ground provisions and oil down. She is strong as an ox but behind her eyes she is but a shell of the vibrant, laughing woman who used to visit us in Brooklyn when I was a child. Aunty Majorie wonders aloud, "You know, sometimes I does wonder how Mummy and Daddy ended up together. They so different."

"Well, you know she cried throughout her entire wedding," I offer, remembering the black-and-white photo of my then eighteen-year-old grandmother with a bouquet large enough to hide the fact that she was pregnant with my mother. It is something we all have wondered. My grandmother and her Catholicism and how she married her husband, a *saga boy*. My grandfather was a good man, for sure, but the idea that my grandmother was pregnant before marriage is something that challenges us all in the family.

This is the last time I saw my grandmother. You were so sad that I had travelled to New York without you. But how could I have taken you? There is so much for me to explain to you. The night I arrived in New York, there was a murder at the bodega on the corner where I stayed while there. How can I explain that in the States, where I have felt my life in danger on more than one occasion, I sometimes feel as though I cannot protect you?

My grandmother's memory is gone. I often wonder if the shame she carried for being an "outside" child is part of what crippled her mind. I also remember the steady supply of pills that my grandmother seemed to be on for years, treating everything from depression to sleeplessness. Perhaps my grandmother too, had demons from her past come knocking on her soul as she got older? I approached my doctor at the time to discuss what I had been experiencing as high-distractibility — and this doctor, with just a questionnaire from the internet, diagnosed me as being depressed.

In Trinidad, the blood of the world, for one reason or another, is in the earth. Our sole existence hinged on how profitable we were first to Spain, then to Great Britain. Europe came through Trinidad, changing hands, sucking this island for whatever profit could be made... Trinidadian life, like that of many other Caribbean islands, was about extraction, production and profit. It was about transforming the sugar cane, the cocoa, later the oil and always the people, into profit. It was about eating the new.

Power belongs to those who make the laws and build the court houses. It belongs to those who have the stamps, the seals, the jails, the money. But even all of this cannot dam the beauty of who we are. In Trinidad and Tobago, like all other colonies of Europe, we must figure out how we will forge a way forward, and we cannot do so until we truly look at our own violent history and forge a separation between who we are and the culture of our oppressors. We cannot afford to hush it away, sweep it under the rug and say, "Shhh, don't talk about that, nah!" In Trinidad and Tobago, we must seek answers in the traditions and customs that were part of our lineage *before* our meeting with Europe, taking from both systems what will work and removing that which will not.

* * *

How many women have had to say "Just forget about it!" to their daughters, knowing that most often, this is the safest option? I mean, even if my mother did go to school and raise hell after I told her about my attack, there are countless stories from the press that reveal that children are still unprotected when it comes to sexual violence.

"Just forget about it."

And my mother.
When she lost her virginity
in a situation which she herself referred to finally, when
she got the words for it,
as date rape,
did she perhaps go to her mother,
who, like her mother before her,
told her to "Just forget about it"

Did my great-grandmother have anyone to turn to?

Recently, I spoke to my mother about this and I asked her why she didn't tell anyone about it. "I don't know," my mother said, "I guess because I was embarrassed." The shame. The silence.

* * *

I don't know any of these things about my great-grandmother as facts. This is all conjecture. I now know, however, that the attack I suffered when I was in the fifth grade triggered a behaviour in me that was destructive. I wish that the adults around me at the time had been better equipped to recognise symptoms of sexual trauma, rather than blaming me and ostracising me, thereby making me more vulnerable to further attacks. As again years later, in Trinidad, when a family member tried to sleep with me, no one in my family believed me except my grandmother and grandfather. No one believed me. And it would be because of death threats from this family member that I would eventually have to leave Trinidad. But Trinidad — like so many other ex-colonies whose inhabitants were brought by violence — surely has a culture of, "just forget about it, nah!"

In this respect, son, we see that countries are not

so different from each other. Whether we talk about Trinidad, Denmark, the United States — there is a constant unwillingness to examine history and to truly understand how we have ended up here and how we could create a different path forward.

Unlike our Western culture, many indigenous cultures around the world have always valued diversity. Diversity isn't just about different skin colour, but about opinions, perspectives, social class. It's about celebrating difference as opposed to imposing conformity. It's about recognising that difference breeds inspiration for growth. We can learn from difference.

I often wonder how my life may have been if I'd had my grandmother to talk to, for even though some of her advice came from fear, it is her humour, vitality and uncompromising love that I miss the most. The last time I saw her she acted very excited, although she did not recognise me. That night she wanted to sleep with me on the pull-out couch in my aunt's living room in Brooklyn.

It was wonderful to sleep next to my grandmother again. As she slept I considered her face and smiled at how little she seemed to age despite her being an octogenarian. Despite her Alzheimer's she seemed to be fit and solid. Her appetite was healthy and she particularly liked to dance to *parang* — the Spanish-inspired Christmas music that we listen to in Trinidad. As she snored I thought about the wise advice she taught me when I was growing up — "Don't eat meat every day" — and her old-fashioned advice: "Wash your panties when you shower so you'll always have a clean pair"; "Sleep with a *tensil* (enamel potty) in your room so you don't have to walk all the way to the toilet." She was my watering hole. She was my tree. She was my guide — my lantern through the darkness of life — and it only seemed fitting that at some point in the middle of the night I woke up, my side warm. I chuckled when I realised she had peed on me, as if claiming me, one last time. Yes, I am my grandmother's.

Many victims of early childhood trauma struggle with healing their pain. In an attempt to understand what I was going through I learned that many victims often exhibited similar symptoms around their thirties — that if untreated could lead to depression, drug use and homelessness. According to a 2012 article by Brooke Axtell entitled "Black Women, Sexual Assault and the Art of Resistance," a study in 2012 by Black Women's Blueprint revealed that "sixty percent of Black girls have experienced sexual abuse before the age of 18." The article continues:

> The pervasive nature of this trauma could translate into an increased risk for Black women and girls to experience depression, PTSD and addiction, common symptoms experienced by many survivors of rape. [...] The Department of Justice estimates that for every white woman that reports her rape, at least 5 white women do not report theirs; and yet, for every African-American woman that reports her rape, at least 15 African-American women do not report theirs.[3]

I wasn't the only victim that day in the gym. I often think about the young boys who perpetuated this violence. Like I mentioned before, one of the only thoughts I can remember having while they were taking my clothes off was that they had certainly seen someone do this to someone else. And I also thought about that woman, too, and the countless others who had to suffer the violence of rape in the past, the present and the future.

We need to call upon the memory of our matriarchs. We need to consult with the totem of the elephant — what can we learn? That not only memory is necessary for survival, but so is intergenerational knowledge.

The Conquest of Kairi: What We Lost in Empire
(A Re-Imagining of the History of Trinidad and Tobago)

because the end of the world has already happen[ed]
— Camae Ayewa, *Fetish Bones*

In the summer of 1498, when the Garini citizens of Cheleide & Aloubaera (Trinidad & Tobago) went down to the seashore in Moruga to lime and boucaner wild meet, they discovered Senor Columbus, the first European tourist, on their beach. Since then, de natives have ben res'less, busy inventing such wonders as a prodigious Street Carnival, Calypso, the Steelpan, Limbo, Roti, perfecting Angostura Bitters, and a philosophy of life that spreads ambiance and goodwill wherever its people go.
— John Mendes, *Cote ci, Cote la: Trinidad & Tobago Dictionary*

Son,

Do you know what your name means?
the ocean in Hawaiian
food in Mauri,
forgiveness in Japanese,
willow in Navajo,
King of Kings in Kono and Kissi (Sierra Leone)

I often wonder what was it like, back *then*?
What was it like, before *them*?

Who were we before *them*?

Why do I speak in the tongue that I do?

What did we get for our ancestral sacrifices?

Tree-lined boulevards and arches
Democratic lies and fascist marches.

They said that their education
would liberate me, but
all it really did
is try to silence me.

It took me far away, from where I come from
Tell me I am nothing and my people are dumb.

9 Sundays of tobacco smoke blown in my face.
9 Sundays of rum sprayed for pain to be erased.
9 Sundays of candles, beads and bush bath.
9 Sundays of dreams to break the aftermath.

Crack

Crack is the sound
that made the whip, All the way from Africa,
in human-stuffed ships.

Crack was the sound
that crystallised in time
cutting it on kitchen tables
a new kind of crime.

Based on survival
to cover up our pain
doing everything in our power
to not go insane.

Crack is the Trap
That caught up with your daddy
made your brother rich
and desecrated your community.

It turned your neighbourhood out
made the pain go away
crack goes the drug–
–the whip of today.

They *dis*covered nothing:

How odd is it that it is the story of a fumbling Genoese that will be remembered as one of heroism and genius, and that he would become the very symbol of European expansionism? Is Columbus named after a dove or a pigeon? The difference is perhaps of some import to this story. And I want you to remember that he is a man whose mother tongue is without a written language.

In his lifetime, Columbus will manage, like his namesake, "the Christ bearer," to carry the weight of the world on his shoulders, but he will buckle, dear son. The Christian world is in trouble — Constantinople kneels before no idols and Prestor John, the Christian King of the East, must be found. But it is in this that Columbus fails — for instead of finding the mysterious Christian King of the East, he finds a people whose existence will forever be changed.

Columbus is as much a hub of intellect as these people are savages. But he is able enough to ensure that his crew reaches terra incognita and he is able enough to ensure their return to the port from which they first sailed. The curious thing about Columbus is he feels God on his side, but if God is on his side, and if God so favours this son of a weaver, then who is on the side of the people of Kairi? It is the Trinity of violence, disease and Christianity that these people must now bow to. God does not make man in his image. Man makes God in his image. And if Columbus is the descendent of weavers, tell me son, what is this tale that he weaves?

Columbus is, we are taught, a capable captain. He is wise enough to understand the power of duplicity. He has, for example, two log books. One is on public view for the sailors to witness, on paper, their accomplishments. The other, the authentic, is hidden in a locked, wooden box, under the captain's bed. Tell me, son, which one do you think will be remembered?

But, before I tell you more, what adventures is Columbus involved in before this fateful journey from what is now called Europe to the world that will be new only to them? Columbus spent time trading in West Africa... played a role in the erosion of people, culture and freedom.

It is interesting to note that we still call this part of the world that he and his men stumbled upon over five hundred years ago the West Indies. It makes me wonder, to the west of whom? The world, after all is a sphere — and who is to say that it is Europe at her centre?

Put yourself in the position of being ashore, on a tropical beach, as Columbus and his ships are first spotted by the indigenous people of what is now called Trinidad. What is it like to stand on shore and behold for the first time these three ships, one of which is named *Naughty Mary*? With white sails billowing out, emerging from the horizon, certainly Columbus' ships must have appeared to be some sort of beast, rising up from the edge of the Earth. We often hear and read of how it was for this motley crew of men to see land, finally, after months of sailing from Spain. We are taught that they were in uncharted territory, supposedly on their way to India. But what about the Kalinago, Carib, Arawak, Tainos? What was it like for them, really, to see these ships approaching for the first time?

As the waves break upon the shore and as certain as the sky is blue above their heads, our ancestors could never have known the fate that was to befall them. For even if they had previously encountered strangers from across the Atlantic — as many historical murmurs attest to — both from the continent of Africa and from Europe, certainly these encounters were never as bloody as this upcoming one would prove to be.

And do not forget the Spain from which Columbus and his crew sail. A Spain taken from the Moors. A Spain enmeshed in the mechanisms that will ensure the obliteration of non-Christians and the seizure of their property and riches.

Our ancestors cannot know their future at this moment. Instead, their bare tamarind- coloured feet are buried in the coolness of the sand. They use their hands to shield their eyes from the glare of the sun as they witness the coming of their plague.

They stand on this beach naked and transfixed. What are these beasts that approach, their wings swelling with the wind? As if sensing the macabre destiny of all the variables in place, the corbeau — or carrion crow — hovers above these ships of destruction.

For each soul, that the Spanish sword is to puncture, is a story that will never be told — the cessation of a heartbeat with its very own rhythm, a dimming of a facet in the tapestry of humanity, forever clouded red by the spill of blood on Earth.

There is a violence that happens here that is as crude as the Spanish swords are sharp. How many ways can you kill a man, a woman or a child? If they do not bring you enough gold, you can, for example, grill them, cut them up, hunt them with dogs that will tear them to pieces, string them up and burn them, throw babies against rocks and into rivers, behead them, rape them.

It matters not how you extinguish their lives, just as long as they are obliterated. Terra nullius? These men from Europe will ensure this.

What strange values these men have.

But this is not what consumes the thoughts of these people who stand here on this beach.

They will not comprehend the ways in which these newcomers conduct their business; they will not comprehend these newcomers' obsession with gold and, most of all, they will not comprehend the barbarity with which they will be treated. It is this failure to grasp the evil that will be unleashed upon them in the name of the cross that will signal their end.

Tell me son, what kind of guest comes into your house, steals your food, rapes your women and murders your brothers? Is this what Europe now fears with the coming of refugees from wars she herself has instigated?

* * *

But how do we remember these people, and why is it important that they be remembered? I say look at the state of Kairi–

Son, I will tell you what I see when I look at the youth in Kairi. The youth from Patna, from Laventille, from Arima, from Couva, San Fernando, San Jaun, Chaguaramus, Diego Martin, Carenage, Covigne Road. If you take the time to look into their eyes, it will take you back to that space between the text and the page of history books written by the hunters. In their eyes, you will see ghosts. If you are still and listen, you will see these ghosts for what they truly are:

our neglected ancestors. They long to be liberated by the beat of a drum whose rhythm is remembered by the order of the universe but forgotten by us all. We must remember the rhythm. We must conjure the rhythm, bring back the rhythm. For what are the ills of this world if not its loss of rhythm? I say let the children and adults who continue our tradition in Best Village, I say son, let them lead the way.

Remember: The conquerors have no rhythm.

The smell of sweet sweat which escapes from sun-touched skin conjures your ancestors. The sourness of the smell is curbed by a child's laugh but it is enough to wake those that sleep beneath the soil. The earth groans and shakes and it trembles with life. They awake from their slumber and remind you of the dreams castrated by the cross. The drums beat. It matters not if it is the beat of an African drum or that of an East Indian drum or the rhythms of the Arawak, Taino or Carib. Together they sing a familiar song but in a language that is not remembered because, long ago, it was silenced by those who lost their rhythm, and dare we say soul?

They dance a dance we strive towards but now are so inarticulate, we cannot go beyond the unfocused grinding and whining to rhythms corrupted with lyrics about the murder of our own, drugs that keep us asleep and fetes that act like opiates. There are ghosts because these ancestors have been forgotten. But we must all remember the Ghost Dance, that movement started in the late 1880s by Wovoka's prophecy, that spread throughout many of the Native American nations. The prophecy, Wovoka revealed, would ensure an end to European expansionism, promote the healing of the Earth and of her people, with the Earth returning to her original, unexploited state. Imagine that a dance is outlawed, which the Ghost Dance was. Tell me son, why would a dance be outlawed?

We were made to forget our ancestors.
We must re-member them.
Put them back together.
Speak their names.
Cast spells of fire &
Take back our land.

It is memory when these same ancestors appear at our every gesture, every breath. Each child born is a portal to the strength of the past. When I look into your eyes you take me there — memory is the blood coursing through your very veins, each minute component handed down from the very beginning, nothing lost, nothing gone, but regenerated and giving new life.

Memory is when the children scorn the sea, because even though they don't say it, their bodies remember the drowning, the desperate attempts of fatigued muscles against the murderous waves of the Atlantic. Their bodies remember the limp carcasses that once belonged to a brother, a sister or even a mother, thrown overboard to the encircling sharks. Their bodies remember their murderous passage from home, to this place of deprivation and depression, a depression in the eyes that remember lost life. Their bodies remember Drexciya, that myth invented by our ancestors of an underwater subcontinent where the unborn children of pregnant African women thrown off slave ships have adapted to breathe underwater. We create ways where there are none.

Memory is when a mother sucks her teeth somewhere in a country in Western Africa and you can hear its echoes throughout the Caribbean. It is eating cassava. It is your grandmother telling you to eat the breadfruit, for were it not for the breadfruit, we would not be here.

"Is slave food," she says, "this is why we still here."

Memory is when our bodies remember the heavy

shackles that were made in England that hold your wrists, tether you by the foot to another who shares your misery, the misery so deep that you know that hell is here on earth. They remember the whips that split and then numb the flesh. They remember the foul excrement of the dungeon, the warm vomit on your toes that turn cold, then from the warmth of your own body, warm again. They remember the ships built in European and American ports. They remember the cut tongue, the castrated father, the way they spit in your face after they rape your mother.

We must never forget.

We must never forget.

Our bodies remember.

* * *

But it is also memory when our children bathe in the sea. How many lineages have been to Maracas? Las Cuevas? Carenage? Chaguaramas? The ancestors tell about the joy too. The joy upon seeing the glance of your child across a field and knowing yes, he is alive, the joy of coupling with a person of your choice and of your body not being discarded. The joy of seeing the okra grow in the same way it grows back in the soil of your village, the joy of learning to read, of being able to say, massah day done gone. The joy of hearing the sweet kaiso, calypso as you chip chip through Port of Spain, eating *channa*, doubles or corn soup and of the generations who learn to bus' a river lime, handed down all the way from India. All this is you, son.

Memory is when children don't like dogs, because they remember. They remember late-night runs through bush, sweat running down hot limbs, dogs after them, as they run for freedom, away from the wrath of enslavement.

Memory cannot be buried. No matter how much you try to forget, memory lingers like the sweet seduction of the lady of the night through the evening of our lives. Memory is unearthed each time you smell lime — it brings you back to the time when your great-grandmother would pick the leaves of the lime tree in the back and make lime bud tea. "Drink it," she says, "it good for yuh."

Each tree that springs forth celebrates the tree before it, every seed that spills forth contains a memory of how things once were and how they will be. Memory is contained within our cells, so that the fruits of our yearnings too remember. Our children celebrate these people who stand on the beach, not knowing their future, the people forced on these boats taken to God only knows where, and those people promised a better life from whence they came. It is memory in the food we grow and the food we cook. The pigeon peas remind us of India, the okra of Africa, the channa of Europe, the cassava of those to whom this land really belongs. From roti to palleau, from boildown to callaloo — each dish tells us of those who danced here before us. What are we all, after all, but the collective memory of some greater force, insisting not to be forgotten? What are we after all but the dreams of our ancestors, a persistent reminder that long ago, our foremothers and forefathers sweat under the hot sun, breaking their backs for the treasury of kingdoms far away and removed, in the cane fields, in the cocoa plantation. What are we anyway, other than a living testimony, a memory, that once the Indian, the African, the Indigenous worked together, laughed together and loved together? But we must learn to listen.

We will remember enough so that we will undo the tree of forgetting — that ritual our ancestors were made to do: circle this tree so we will forever forget Africa. Circle this tree so that we will not remember the colluders whose souls were corrupted by alcohol (Arabic *al-kuhl*, "the kohl" — the hole), guns and power. We cast off this spell:

We are still here and we remember.
We will not forget that which has been done to us
& we shall balance the book of life.

You see, Kairi is about Memory. It is about not forgetting the people who stood naked, on that beach, that fateful day that Columbus stumbled upon them and wiped the sunshine out of their lives, forever. It is about not forgetting the people who were kidnapped and enslaved for hundreds of years. It is about not forgetting who we were before the curse of the cross. Memory is the possibility inherent in the richness of our souls. When we forget, we die. And that is why the youth must dig. They must dig and dig and find the memories that make them because we have forgotten who we are. And the youth? They must remember in order to live. They must remember the rhythm. They must remember our ancestors.

Remember: The year is 1498 when their eyes first fall upon the stumbling strangers from the sea. It will take some years for the discordant vibrations of Spain to develop and gain momentum through the waters, until like a tsunami it washes its destruction upon the island Kairi and her people. To be sure, they had heard of them. Nothing is stagnant throughout these islands. Information such as the previous journeys of these men has spread with the exchange of fruit, meat and women, men and children. And it is with much curiosity that these people who will later be called Arawak stand there on that beach. They wonder, of course, what do these men bring with them this time?

But these brown-skinned people have yet to learn that the only thing these newcomers bring with them is their violence and their greed. Despite these things to come however, they meet these strangers from the sea as any other civilised people would — in peace and hospitality. When a ship needs to be repaired, they give them the tar from their lake. When hunger and heat howl hungrily at their health, they share their cassava and corn. When the men, in health, grow restless, the women even give themselves.

The weathered travellers, encouraged by their captain, believe themselves to be on the doorstep of Eden — where else can these men, most common by birth, receive the riches of the Earth so freely, so copiously and so willingly? Clearly these sea-beaten conquerors have never seen the spirit of humanity, in the way they experience it through these brown brothers and sisters of these islands.

But that is not what is of concern to them who are indigenous to Kairi. What is of concern to them is how best to rid themselves of this pale plague and resume life as they once knew it. Because like all groups of people who come upon another foreign group, these indigenous people, no matter how hospitable they are, cannot rid themselves of this one simple fact: the new arrivals smell.

But from the moment the dark eyes of even one of these indigenous people fall upon these wasted wretches, their story, their very existence, becomes irrevocably shaken. Their fate becomes entwined with that of this blundering sailor and the greedy and desperate kingdoms from which these men come. Their lives and stories, like a sapling at the bottom of a rainforest, become blanketed and dwarfed by the darkness above. This darkness from the sea signals their Armageddon.

We cannot forget that there was no paradise here when dark eyes fell upon the bearers of gunpowder and disease, true, but what must not be forgotten is that there was no genocide either.

Whether they were in what is now called the Americas, Africa or India — at least not on the scale Europe brings to these shores.

Years before stumbling upon this so-called New World,

the Portuguese had already penetrated the western coast of Africa and brought home gold dust, strange fruits and African slaves. They beat back the bush like a lion tamer with a whip and leave but nothingness in their wake. They conduct business with others who cannot fathom the destiny of this trade. They infiltrate and destabilise slowly, imperceptibly at first. In this continent that is called Africa, humanity's vanity falls to its knees in the presence of alien creations and lives are exchanged for glass beads, caps and clothes that hang suspect on the new owner's skin. The story is one that will become a capitalist one — lives exchanged for trinkets.

Portugal dominates the global stage then. Columbus, married to the daughter of a Portuguese nobleman, is witness to the rise of this empire. It is a convenient marriage for them both — he procures access to the Royal Court and her family receives, hopefully, relief from their poverty.

The exploration of the Atlantic and the pushing back of the horizon is in the air. The magnitude of the destruction cannot be reckoned with, especially among a people whose greed supersedes their fear of death. Fortresses are built and Portugal's only real enemy is not the people who inhabit this coast, but from within; therefore, she cannot look without.

Fast-forward and so Columbus enters Spain a thirty-four-year-old widowed destitute. He will not make history until he is thirty-nine. Columbus' success hangs on serendipity: Spain fights the crescent with the cross and sweeps its Jews out of its way. What is at stake in the end is not the amount of gold, nor even how large the empire. What is at stake, in the end, is the way in which history is written. Like a jealous sister, Spain is bent on eclipsing her sister Portugal. Spain is interested in Columbus' ideas, but she is distracted. He approaches Portugal yet again, but this time at the height of her African triumph. Columbus finds that Portugal, having found the sea route to the Indies along Africa's coast, is now in want of nothing. Truly it can be said that one man's discovery is (wittingly or unwittingly), the other man's destruction. But he does not allow himself to be destroyed. Spain continues her battle against the Moors, where even Isabella herself dons armour and sword. Granada falls and a spirit of invincibility intoxicates the Spanish crown enough to give in to the folly of Columbus.

So, in the end Columbus sets sail to convert the heathens he already assumes are out there, while hopefully fattening the purse of the Spanish treasury. In his possession is a letter of introduction from the King and Queen of Spain, which in their minds the people to be encountered will of course comprehend; a crude compass that is not reliable and the crew of ninety or so men who are disgruntled to be under the command of a foreigner.

For a foreigner Columbus is. Remember, he is Genoese and like his crew, he has his prejudices. Interestingly enough, there are claims that he even hails originally from Corsica. Supposedly, you can visit his house in Calvi! How Corsica comes back to us, washes ashore on our lives! But let's move on: Venetians, as far as he is concerned, cannot be trusted, although it is Marco Polo he adores. But when the Spanish Court grants Columbus his wish it, of course, does it at another's expense. The town of Palos would be so honoured to supply Columbus with two ships and a crew. Its citizens hear of this honour in a former mosque, now church, at a mass. From Palos were given the ships *Niña* and *Pinta* — the girl and the whore. But let us not forget Santa Maria's humble beginnings — first as *Naughty Mary* and then to *Holy Mary*. But foreigner or not, Columbus is successful in launching, finally, his dream — this journey to Cipan Guó, which promises to make him Admiral of the Sea and, rich.

From its port, he sails to the Canary Islands, the ancient land of the Guanches, the people of Tenerife, who years before having suffered the very same fate their so-called New World brothers and sisters are now destined to face. For is it not one of the universal aspects of humanity, Europe likes to teach us, to conquer, or be conquered?

Kairi, or Trinidad, as it has been called since the sighting of it, finds itself in the predicament of being part of Spain's vastly growing empire. Just like an empire with too many mouths to feed, Spain neglects those that are not as productive as the others. Mexico is doted upon like the firstborn, while others, with uses yet to be discovered, lay neglected and left to their own devices.

The Spaniards plant a port where Conquerabia once lay and name it the Port of the Spaniards, forever to be abbreviated to POS, of which your own grandfather once noted, "Yes, piece of shit."

The Spanish manage to dispossess Guanagares — a Carib chief in Trinidad — and his people and attempt, in their way, to extract something useful from this island. They live in straw huts and depend on those indigenous to the land to feed them. Do not bite the hand that feeds you until you are fat enough to slaughter it.

It takes a few months for any letters to reach Spain and, once there, they are never answered.

It is illegal for the Spaniards to trade with other nations, but again, Spain is not there to supply this outpost, and without trade what are these settlers to do without the basic necessities of civilisation: cloth, bullets and knives? But luckily, the British and Dutch make willing participants in a trade that is illegal and the consequences dire — many an indigenous person is known to have been hanged and quartered for trading with English ships.

There is fighting, of course, between the Spaniards who are there and the people who were already there and suddenly the latter take on a schizophrenic description in the books of these Spaniards. To the Spaniards, there are two types of indigenous people: the Arawak and the Caribs — and for centuries later, little Black boys and girls who will be called West Indian will learn from their textbooks that the Arawak were peaceful and the Caribs were cannibals. It is a passing on of information that is never questioned, passed on from the parent, unquestioningly, to the child who receives it, unquestioningly. We grow up under the same skies, perhaps the same trees and eat cassava, sweet potatoes, avocados without ever knowing, really knowing...

But what of these people and what did the Spaniards mean, when they called some hostile and some friendly? Flipped, as all history should be, one can see that there was certainly only one type of Indian — those who come from India — but then again, there are so many different types of Indians. But for the Spaniards there were two types of indigenous people — those that corroborated with the Spaniards and those that fought for their freedom and their dignity. Heroes to those of this island; criminals, of course, to the Spanish.

But there is a weapon that they have against the Spanish. It may take months for messages to reach Spain, but it is a matter of weeks for messages to reach throughout this old world. Drums and cries carry messages of a great kingdom that is felled at the hands of a Spaniard, a Spaniard who spills blood at the sight of gold. Gold: it is all these Spaniards ask for and soon these indigenous people learn the convenience of not having any gold, and sending the Spanish away, to over there, where there always will be plenty. And so, a myth is birthed, pulled out of the memories of these people and together they begin to spin a tale, a tale of a golden cacique, where mountains are capped with diamonds and mines are full of gold. And this place, this city of gold, this El Dorado? Always point the Europeans away from the ones you love.

The Lament of Lanzarote

In fact, as a woman, I have no country. As a woman
I want no country. As a woman, my country is the
whole world.
— Virginia Woolf, *Three Guineas*

Son,

I cannot explain why although I may feel more at home in
some places than others, I feel an inexplicable connection to
the whole world. I've never liked national flags. I've always
shied away from declaring nationalities and have always felt
that the world would be a better place if this was common
practice.

Although I have always enjoyed travelling, there is a
kind of awkwardness about it that I have not truly been
able to liberate myself from, and that is the ability to travel
off the beaten path. Our trip to Lanzarote cemented for me
why it was necessary for me to travel more untraditionally,
and not in the usual touristy tradition that, although safe,
can also be a bit asphyxiating as well.

We left Denmark during *Efterårsferie* — fall vacation —
that week that we get off in October. It is a remnant of
the days of farming, when children were needed at home
to help harvest potatoes. I find it very interesting to see
the role that potatoes play in Danish and, by extension,
European cuisine. It's interesting to note that the potato is
not indigenous to Western Europe and that of all the ground
provisions to bring back from the so-called New World, the
potato, as we know it today, in Europe anyway, is amongst

the least nutritious of them all. It wasn't even brought to Europe until 1536. I'm an armchair agricultural traveller, often revelling in the fact that so many foods we take for granted as part of national cuisines aren't even indigenous to these countries. Take for example tomatoes, which we have all come to identify with Italian food, but which also come from South America. It would be nice if we could be as open with people as we are with certain agricultural products!

When you have grown up in the Caribbean with a grandmother who still has the soil of the Earth in her heart, you learn about ground provisions such as yams, eddoes, dasheen. But these foods are difficult to find here — requiring a bit of effort through the dark winter rains — and my diet too follows the time of the day and includes plastic-covered bananas being cultivated by enslaved workers perhaps, and coconut water that comes in boxes. I often long for the days of living in Trinidad and being able to pick mangoes from trees and drink coconut water from actual coconuts — for free!

Luckily, we're able to escape the grey of autumn in Denmark into a sunny part of the world, where we can cheat our way into sun. Summer, even. The problem with travelling in our capitalist world, where countries are offered up on websites to be bought, is that you can end up somewhere that does not fit you. Now, it's never really the terrain, the land per say, that you will not feel you belong to — but the particular slice of society you may have inadvertently landed in. An aspect of being a writer is that your curiosity can take you far beyond what you know, and you can land in all sorts of unlikely places. The point is there is a fine balance between my true literary curiosity for life and what it is I truly find comfortable. And going to Lanzarote with your ten-year-old self taught me a lot about that.

* * *

One learns early whether one is an independent traveller or a group traveller. And although I have already known for quite some time that I am an independent traveller (I first travelled alone as a baby from Brooklyn to Trinidad) I was now travelling with you, and so as a parent. This wasn't the first trip I'd taken with you, but it certainly was the first trip where we'd travelled to a place previously unknown to me. Travelling with a child presents its own challenges. The most important one is that the place is interesting enough not only to myself, but to you as well — and for me, Lanzarote, with its volcanic landscape and warm weather, presented such a place.

It was time that I tried the inexpensive package deals. The ones that offer Scandinavians solar relief from the darkness. I picked Lanzarote because it looked ruggedly beautiful, in an intergalactic kind of way, *and it is*. It reminded me of Mars — and you know me, I have a thing for Mars, having blogged as "Blackgirl on Mars" for years at this point. I managed to get a pretty decent rate for the tickets and hotel.

By now, you've been to the Canary Islands countless of times with your father. But back then, it would be your first time. I knew I could get my Caribbean weather fix, hear Spanish, get out of Denmark and be close to the spot that played no a small part in Columbus launching the seeds of European imperialism out into the world. I became particularly interested in the Canary Islands when once, during a bout of researching, I discovered that there was an indigenous group there and that they too were conquered, colonised, but now are barely perceptible amidst the lineage of the people there. I became intrigued by the Guanches of the Canary Islands because, throughout my travels around the world, one thing made itself particularly clear: we are not as far away from each other as we think we are.

A great example of this is housing: whether you're in Hawaii, the Caribbean, the southern US, South America, Africa, you will see that there is a pattern there. In these places, you will find galvanised rooftops, concrete houses, verandas, and louvers: all clues of the Europeans adjusting to tropical climes. If you come from a country that has once been colonised by a certain European country, well, chances are you have just as much in common with that European country and her other former colonies as you do with your biological "ethnic" ancestors. Meaning, I may be of East Indian and African heritage but due to my Western cultural heritage/indoctrination, I seem to know way more about the continent of Europe than either India or Africa.

* * *

So Lanzarote. I was excited. You and I looked at pictures of it on the Internet for days, commenting on its black, volcanic landscape and vast expanse of ocean. When we land, the heat that hits us as we deplane takes me back to the Caribbean. Ah, I am home, I think.

As we drive in the taxi to our hotel, your smile is as large as the sky, and we can't help but wonder at the whitewashed houses glittering like diamonds against their backdrop of black lava-covered landscape. The sky is blue and the hotel, once we arrive, sprawling. It's always a good time to travel when the economy is bust. Prices go down as the wise hold on tighter to their money. It is the fools who fuel the economy.

So for a very modest price you and I could stay in a five-star hotel, with an ocean-view and three-resident swimming pools. After we enter the hotel room, we immediately raid the fridge for goodies. We bounce on the bed and contemplate the lavish hotel compound and the sparkling, blue sea.

Lanzarote is, indeed, magical. The staff, gracious. We soon learn of the grounds of Puerto Calero, and walk along the promenade to the small town. We enjoyed the fact that we are out of Denmark and that the weather is fantastic. There isn't much to do the first day we arrive except discover our neighbouring town. Fortunately for us, it is populated with a few good places to eat. We survive on pizza our entire time there, and you experience me for what will regrettably not be the last time entering a state of shopping frenzy in a clothing store. While in Lanzarote, I cornrow my hair and, once finished, you look at me with awe and say, "Wow! You can really do that?" That night, before we sleep and wake up to start the day with the breakfast buffet, you and I look up at the sky and it is as if the stars are all sparkling for us. The perspective of the night sky, from that location and time of year, is spectacular. I show you the Pleiades star constellation, which resembles an arrow, and from that I can discover, for the first time, Orion.

In an attempt to sustain whatever connection you may still have to the universe, I have begun taking more of an interest in all things nature. But this ends up being pathetic disparate attempts at gathering information from the Internet in a life not yet fully able to contemplate its own existence. How can I catch you, while I feel as though I am falling?

It was around this time I started to become like, what is really going on in the world? What are we all doing here? Why are we running around like we know what this is all about, but don't? Nobody does! What is the meaning of life?

I start thinking, imagine if everybody in the whole world just stopped. I envision every single human being stopping what they are doing — no shopping, no television, no school, no work, getting off their computers, turning the TV off, putting that hoe down in the field kind of thing and come together. Come together and decide to do things differently. That instead of profit being the bottom line, we'll make the welfare of the planet and the life she sustains our priority. We won't leave it to philosophers or other people of science, we're not going to hand it over to religion, and we're not going to leave it to politicians. Instead, we're going to consider each other and ourselves, the planet and the destruction our culture is responsible for. We'll make LIFE our focus. It'll be like a world-wide Contemplate Life day, except it won't be just one day, it will be our priority, till we get it right.

But until then, I attempt to squeeze my contemplation of life in between teaching, raising you and navigating life in a foreign country. Why does everything have to be so alienated from the other? Why does everything have to be so splintered? So, I endeavour to decode the skies and stars. I plot all the full moons into my calendar for the rest of the year. This I do in Lanzarote. You admit that the constellations are magnificent. I do think you manage to get the enormity of it, just enough to snap yourself from the iPod stupor you seemed to be in at the time.

So that night we rest, you and I, in Lanzarote, thinking, hey, we certainly beat the system this time! From the middle of the Danish darkness, we have escaped south...

I realised, while living here, how important it is for me to see *difference*. But when you live in a country that was cited by the right-wing Norwegian Anders Behring Breivik —who blew up a building in Oslo, Timothy McVeigh-style, murdering eight people, and later the same day shot dead sixty-nine Norwegians, many of them children, on the island of Utøya — in his white-supremacist manifesto as one of the only two European countries to have it right (read: anti-immigration policies firmly in place) then you get my drift. To put it mildly: I rarely even wear my hair out in this place.

So travelling has become a kind of cure for this. I have

used Copenhagen as my European base to see, well, more of Europe. It is in this spirit that I would travel to London and experience a multiculturalism I thought only existed in New York, or Trinidad for that matter, and would take you along with me. I'll never forget how overwhelmed I felt by all the people on Oxford Street and how amazed we both were by the diversity there. It is in this spirit that I travelled to Madrid and wondered at its obvious opulence. It was in this spirit that I travelled to Berlin with you, only to be overpowered by the architecture that can only have been designed to make human beings feel, well, *small*. It was in this spirit that I travelled along with Adrianne George and her Black Women in Europe social network to Amsterdam, and revelled in the First Annual Black Women in Europe Festival, and fell in love with the Surinamese people, recognising my Caribbean roots in their food, their faces, and their spirits.

The next day in Lanzarote at the breakfast buffet, you lean in towards me and whisper, "Mom, we *really* stand out here." And you're right. Here we are, yet again, although far from Copenhagen, sticking out. I with my colourful scarves and flip flops, among men with boating shoes and women with pearls, you with your eyes jumping playfully and challengingly at me. It is true that I belong to no country but the world. Yes, I belong to that, and no right-wing nationalist ideology will every change that.

The Birth of a Mother

Son,

Like so many other women who become mothers, I have to admit that I lost myself. Don't get me wrong, the first few years of mothering you as a baby were some of the best years of my life. Every time I hear a baby cry, my heart aches and I think about when you were so new into this world, and we spent all of our time together. At the time when folks would tell me how fast it would go, I would think not fast enough! Oh, how foolish I was back then! How fast it goes!

Most of the time, I was relieved, to be honest, that the only thing I had to focus on was you. My usually erratic self was calm in your early years. I was grounded, had purpose, and although I experienced some of the fear and confusion that can inevitably be a part of parenthood, the immediacy of your presence didn't leave much room to give in to that.

However, there comes a time in a mother's life when she must find her way back to herself, to who she was before motherhood, take it up again, like a stitch on a knitting needle, and work it into the life she now finds herself in. There comes a time when we must remember, in case we forgot, our dreams, wishes and hopes. It could be easy to lose yourself in conversations about diaper sales, if you're not too careful. Don't get me wrong: I didn't want to entirely go back to who I was before I had you — change is always a good thing and I hope that I will always be able to grow for as long as live — but I certainly didn't want to disregard the parts of me that were worth keeping, like my curiosity for life and my writing.

Throughout the years here in Denmark, there have been many women whose existence has brought me life, laughter and relief.

I've met a lot of Sarahs in my life and have gotten along with all of them. But this Sarah I'm telling you about wasn't really named Sarah. Her name was Mandana. "Like Banana," she told me, as her emerald-speckled dark eyes shone. And we laughed like we were both twelve and smoking cigarettes in the school's bathroom, rather than two women in a foreign land combating the alienation and isolation that is a part of that.

I met her eighteen months into the new land of motherhood and Denmark. Due to the comprehensive healthcare system here, I could stay home with you (thank you, Denmark!). But once you received a spot in the local *vuggestuen* (day-care), I would have to begin my process of integration. I would become *activated* and would begin the process of learning Danish.

For me to operate anywhere close to what I had done professionally in New York, learning Danish was a must, of course. I found it terribly difficult to learn Danish in the beginning. The only other language I knew was Trinidadian patois — which the inattentive would call broken English, but with its own syntax it may as well be another language. It was my mother tongue and took no conscious effort to learn. Whenever I attempted Danish, however, I felt disabled in a way that was challenging for me to navigate atop the other issues of immigrant living and motherhood that I found myself wading through. And whenever I did try to speak Danish, you hated it and demanded I speak English to you. I do understand this — no child likes to hear his or her parents stumble and fumble in a foreign tongue. We are supposed to be the authority, and many can rarely be that in another tongue other than their own.

After eighteen months at home with you, I was ready to see what Denmark was all about. I'd met the country thus far through your father and I liked it. Your father's Denmark consists of a Christianshavn that was working-class rather than the gentrified hotspot it has become. His Denmark was openness and freedom. That is why I decided to stay. Through your father I met a crew of folks who upheld old-school Danish ideals such as socialism. I learned that Carlsberg and Tuborg were both pilsners that were as different as Coke and Pepsi, and Carib and Stag in Trinidad. As mentioned, I learned about Kierkegaard's favourite spot in Gilleleje, and that people from Copenhagen teased those from Jutland in very much the same way Trinidadians teased Tobagonians or Grenadians, or people from Manhattan teased folks from Brooklyn. Sometimes we're not so different from each other, after all. I learned that Denmark had a particular talent for engineering and functional perfection that is reminiscent of a Japanese or even German aesthetic. I learned through your grandmother, your father's mother, who you lovingly refer to as "your goddess," what love and patience felt like when she not only opened her home to me, but taught me to knit, something I had always wanted to learn, while you were nestled comfortably in my womb. Denmark thus far had been cool to me.

But I still had not met anyone who knew about James Baldwin. I had yet to meet anyone who knew anything about the racial legacy of the West, including Denmark. I hadn't met anyone who knew who bell hooks was or Jamaica Kincaid. In short, I had not met anyone who shared the same cultural and intellectual interests as me. This doesn't mean that they weren't out there, I just hadn't met them yet.

I went to a language school out in the neighbourhood of Nordvest, not that far from my neighbourhood of Vesterbro. Nordvest is very different from the neighbourhood we lived in at the time, as it's more known for its large immigrant population. While many neighbourhoods in Copenhagen look quaint and like something out of fairy tales, there are many parts of Nordvest that were not as charming, in looks anyway. There's a bustling multi-ethnic population with an elevated train station that reminded me of Brooklyn. Every morning I would bike to your *vuggestuen* in Vesterbro — you in your bike seat secured to my bike — down the beaten-up street of Sundevedsgade, over to the other side of Vesterbro, past the drug addicts and sex shops on Istedgade, and after you drove off in your bus to the countryside, I would then bike out to Nordvest. Every morning, no matter if it was raining or snowing. Then, at two o'clock when I was done with school, I'd bike back, pick you up and take you home.

I was happy for a little change of scenery although not too thrilled to leave you in day-care. While Denmark does have a day-care system many countries would envy, I can't help but think that the institutionalisation happens too early, too fast. According to a recent article, Denmark holds the world's record in the high degree in which we institutionalise our children, surpassed perhaps only by North Korea.[1] But I realise that, as a mother who lives in a country where childcare is not as much of an issue as it would be for me in the States, my critique is perhaps a luxury. However, one wonders what the social impact of this will be in the future.

Most of the architecture and design in Copenhagen is spectacular — whether it's the new opera house or the Black Diamond which houses the Royal Library, or even the little candy-coloured houses of Christianshavn that are hundreds of years old, it's not uncommon to stop in wonder at many of the architectural gems that bejewel this city. Even the police stations and post offices have designer lamps. There are, however, a few pimples here and there. I was sitting in one and it felt as though this pimple was about to pop.

Architecture determines behaviour? This building did not inspire learning.

On the first day, I found the classroom and saw my future classmates all waiting outside the locked door. From a cursory glance I saw scarves covering heads and an energy I could recognise from childhood of adults in foreign territory; adults who look like life is about to cascade down upon them. Not all immigrants emit this energy. Not the ones who are robust enough, after settling in, to be able to attack life with the tenacity being an immigrant requires. Remember now: it is not good enough to work just as well as your co-worker/classmate/host-country citizen. You have to work *twice* as hard. These students had not, like my father, given up. Not yet. I could tell by their very presence that there was something in them that sparkled. It felt very much like hope.

I have learned a lot about the world by moving to Denmark. And it all really started in this classroom. Before, I didn't know anything about Iran other than the Iran hostage crisis, which occurred when I was a child living in Brooklyn. All I really got from what I'd learned back then, though, was that Iran was supposed to be our enemy. I remember seeing people with buttons that read, "Fuck Iran." But my interest, as a child, was not in politics — for no matter who the president was, he never seemed to be a friend of Black people. Besides, I had more interesting things, at least to me, to contend with, like learning how to straighten my hair with a hot comb in India's kitchen. Meeting Sarah, however, and being in this class gave me a better understanding of the world, and through her, what had happened in Iran.

* * *

When I lived in Trinidad, it didn't take long to understand

how many were not fans of what was felt to be American interventionism. Although many Trinidadians would migrate to the US for work and more upward social mobility, there was still a core who were suspicious of the US military-industrial complex. There's a saying in the Caribbean that if America sneezes, the Caribbean catches pneumonia. When I first moved to Trinidad, there was only one television channel that signed on at noon and signed off in the early evening. Many of the shows we received were from the States — outdated episodes of *Sesame Street* and daytime soap operas. The US dominated the media, much like they do here in Denmark. From pop icons to designer labels, the US always had a strong cultural presence, much to the chagrin of many who saw it as just another face of imperialism.

I think that what a lot of Danes I have encountered primarily don't like about the US is its foreign policy. But again, right at the time I arrived — and still now — many Danes were made to witness, in a slow motion that was going too fast, their government transforming from one of the most socially progressive in the world to one that now is in the midst of beefing up its military.

Being against the foreign policy of the United States was not something I hadn't heard before. Growing up in the Caribbean between one generation that saw freedom near (my grandfather's generation), another that fell asleep on it (my mother's generation) and a third that ran from it (my generation), American foreign policy was something that directly affected our lives. Whether it was the US military base building roads and inspiring the lyrics to Mighty Sparrow's "Jean & Dinah" proclaiming, "Yankee gone and Sparrow take over town!," I grew up with a ping-ponging of opinions from churches to gallery limes to rum shops to beach limes. Criticism of US foreign policy was common to any child growing up in Trinidad in the Eighties and the

Nineties, at a time when economic freedom was not just a possibility but appeared to be a political reality. I lived in Trinidad when Maurice Bishop was murdered, and witnessed how many did not appreciate the involvement of the US in the affairs of Grenada.

Ever since arriving here I couldn't help but notice that, politically, Denmark seemed to be stepping into the shoes of Brigitte Nielsen to the US's very Sylvester Stallone Rambo-like stance in world politics.

On that first day of class, I noticed the book, an autobiography, that Sarah held in her hands, before I saw her. The book was *Assata*: *An Autobiography* by Assata Shakur. I studied the cover and was grateful to see this image of a powerful Black woman staring back at me. I thanked the ancestors and followed the slender fingers and military-jacketed arm that held the book. Her face was the shape of an olive which was quite fitting because it was the colour of her eyes. Her hair was short — shorter on one side and sticking up in the middle. She was wearing the quintessential anarchist uniform of combat boots and black slender jeans.

Sarah, who hails from Canada, and I end up being the only two Westerners in the class. The other classmates were from Iraq, Afghanistan, Iran, Turkey and other countries in what we call the Middle East. Our teacher, a Danish woman, seemed to be going through post-traumatic stress disorder. She always held a plastic cup of coffee in her shaky hands, and she sucked on cigarettes during breaks like they were somehow a source of oxygen. Our other teacher was a Turkish man who wore leather pants and bore an uncanny resemblance to Freddie Mercury.

Many of the stories of my classmates were heart-breaking. There was an Iraqi father of four, a computer specialist, without a job or a home. He'd sent out a scores of CVs and never received a response. There was a female gynaecologist from Afghanistan who, because of my many years of Catholic guilt programming, I was totally convinced would hate me for being American — though, luckily, life is not a television show. Her name was Gora and she was a female force who inspired me through her gentle laughter and generosity of spirit. There was Tariq, the young man from Pakistan, Hussein from Iran... everyone far from home, all speaking English with an accent, all speaking much better Danish than both Sarah and me. Sarah and I soon would learn, however, that we were different.

Through my growing friendship with Sarah, I learned that her mother was French Canadian and her father Iranian. Although she never told me too much about her personal life I did know that her relationship to her father, like mine, was complicated. There are no cultural monopolies on controlling and authoritative men. Sarah was also gay. She, like me, had gotten her residency here through her marriage. Sarah was learning, just like me, that married life wasn't necessarily for everyone. It would be great if marriage wasn't a prerequisite for being together, as sometimes happens in many transnational relationships.

What I re-learned from Sarah through my friendship with her in that class was just how much the work of Audre Lorde provided a source of strength for us as women, and how much it spoke to our own personal experiences. She also introduced me to the work of Marjane Satrapi, and to the work of Mary Daly, who had an unfortunately contentious relationship with Lorde, and by some accounts did not even engage with this powerful poet and thinker, demonstrating the tension that is often present in white feminism. But it was through Daly that I learned about the power, history, strength and gender discrimination inherent in words like *strange*, *weird* and *witch*.

Sarah and I shared photocopied books of herbs whose medicinal uses, if more widely known, would be enough to put the pharmaceutical companies out of business. We talked about how the medical industry was based on the genocide of female healers during the hundreds of years of femicide in Europe. We talked about how the plague in Europe could have been facilitated by the widespread murdering of cats that was a part of the witch hunts. We talked about the hypocrisy of the West and how it erases other cultures such as Iran and indigenous knowledges from Africa and throughout the world. We were both relieved to, for the first time since moving to Denmark, meet someone else who didn't mistake the name bell hooks for a fishing store. Together, Sarah and I did what so many women before our time and after will continue to do: we taught each other about our own respective experiences in life in the body politic that we have been born into, knowing that through this sacred and age-old cultivation of knowledge of the other we were also building our own integrity into the wholeness of the human story.

We could have been working on some exquisite beading in a tent somewhere in the hills of Afghanistan. We could have been gathering wood in a forest of Russia. We could have been standing side by side, ready for battle, in Angola. The point is that we were women and women have always come together for our very own survival, and being with Sarah created an energy that kept that real for me. While a mother was born when I gave birth to my son, my intellect was reborn upon meeting Sarah. She saved me.

But we were sitting in a fluorescent-lit classroom with a teacher who drank way too much coffee and who may have been my first introduction to the state of shocked womanhood. We were sitting in a classroom where we were the only two Westerners. It is true that we were women. It is true that I am, politically, Black, and Sarah biracial and gay. But that did not matter there. Suddenly, our Western-ness was all that mattered. The school did not know what to do with us. They were used to the paternal relationships that they felt were necessary to the idea of help, assistance, charity — call it what you will — between the system and countries they deemed, incorrectly, to be backwards, like Iran, Afghanistan and other Middle Eastern countries. There was no room in their ideas of help for the rich histories of these countries. Sarah and I were a monkey wrench in this narrative: they had to vomit the anomaly of us as quickly as they could back into Danish society!

Sarah and I progressed at lightning speed through this Danish programme, although we both didn't really speak Danish conversationally the way we wanted to be able to. Sarah, who already spoke French and Farsi, definitely began commanding the language better than I, but there was a steady sadness that many moving to Denmark seem to be crippled by. I think what a lot of people are not prepared for is how little the sun shines here and how distant Danish culture can be. It is not uncommon for melanated folks to get a vitamin-D deficiency. I have it. Together we joked about her insistence on wearing black clothes, her laughter always falling upon my ears as such a relief, as I felt understood, accepted and valued for who I was.

We often thought about and spoke about the preferential treatment we seemed to experience at the school and how weird it was to feel privileged in a way that we had never before experienced. We both joked that we "felt white," knowing exactly what we meant when we said this. It was weird for both of us to think that, for the first time in our lives, we found something about our identities that seemed to "work" for rather than against us, while at the same time realising that there was something seriously broken in the system in order for things to have unfolded in the way they did. We saw how the relationship between power, statehood and migration all congealed into a parallel existence for so many that seems virtually impossible to escape despite their credentials, qualifications, hopes and dreams.

Sarah and I eventually made our way out of that school. We learned that if you had a college education that was recognised in Denmark (read: from a Western country) you could go to another school, an even better school where rumour had it students were zipping through in months, being able to pass the state-certified Danish exams in a year — qualifying to operate professionally supposedly on the level you once did in your home country.

We parted ways, Sarah's Danish being so much more advanced than mine that she quickly went ahead of me. I started at level one and learned that the school I now found myself in was developed by the US military to teach its men and women Vietnamese during the war. Except now we're using it to learn Danish. Great. As I looked around my new classroom full of savvy Europeans, Americans and the products of phantom immigrations such as myself, I grew a little bit sad. Sitting in the ultra-cool neighbourhood of Nørrebro (which gets a lot of its "cool" from its diversity), I wondered about the other students I had left behind in the not-so-pretty neighbourhood of Nordvest, where the train station took me back to childhood memories of Flatbush. I wondered about my former classmates and the desperation so many of them had on their faces — perhaps a desperation to be a part of something meaningful. To be let in. I didn't see people who didn't want to work. I saw people running from war. From bombs dropped on their homes by Western governments. I wondered about Tariq and whether he was able to get the job at the restaurant he wanted so desperately; I wondered whether Gora would ever be able to practice as a gynaecologist here.

I went on to meet other students. But I would never really shake that experience of sharing a space with these men and women who were all here in Denmark, trying to do what every other human being in this world desires —

and that is to live. And for this, they will always be my heroes.

I miss Sarah.

Denmark's Real National Treasures

Son,

I know that being a child of immigrants can be challenging. I know, because I am one. I've seen you see me navigate through foreign territory. I remember when I was a child noticing how my mother would wear summer dresses in winter or speak with what I felt to be her loud accent on the train and becoming so embarrassed by this. I've witnessed you experiencing some of the same discomfort with me. I remember trying my best to distance myself as much as I could from all of the cringe-worthy situations my parents seemed to subject me to and become more like my American friends. Being a child of immigrants often means that you become interpreter, not only of languages but cultural codes as well. How many times have I asked you what a particular Danish word means?

Through my parents I learned much of staple Trinidadian culture like bake, calypso, and the long list of words that seem peculiar to our culture such as *maco*, short for "macoscious" a Trinidadian word that means you're being nosey or to describe something that is too much, like a big *maco* bus or a big *maco* house. Through me my parents were introduced to double-dutch, cornrows and, much to their chagrin, bubble gum and a loud mouth. They learned the background (albeit false) to some of the American holidays that were being celebrated all around them, like Thanksgiving, through their children. And although being a child of immigrants often renders you low on the hierarchical structure in your neighbourhood there are many ways to offset this: through excellence, whether in academics or sports. I did both when I was young and experienced how this excellence was quickly rewarded with respect from my classmates, teachers and parents.

In the States, although I was the child of immigrants, I am American. I was born in Brooklyn and even though I had spent some time in Trinidad already at a young age, my family let me know that I was the Yankee girl. It was something my grandmother was quite proud about, as though my family had won a grand prize. By the time I returned to the States after living in Trinidad from the ages of eleven to fifteen I landed in a high school at Union Square in Manhattan. And although this school would be one of the first high schools in the US to get equipped with metal detectors back in the Eighties, I and many others still managed to excel there. Despite the school's reputation, Washington Irving High School had a core of excellent teachers and students and I learned much about New York City in that school.

Here in Denmark, however, being born in this country doesn't seem to be a guarantee that you are Danish. Just this past year a debate was launched where lines seemed to have been drawn between ethnic Danes, meaning white, and children born to parents who were from other, mostly Middle Eastern countries. But when I ask you what you are, you tell me with confidence that you are Danish. Your whole crew of friends reflect the many hues and colours of the human race and they too are Danish.

Around 2010 I was headhunted to teach at a private school in Vesterbro, Copenhagen. This school is one in which I had always wanted to work from the moment I first walked through its doors four years prior to that. The group of children had faces that reflected every corner of the globe. The kids, thankfully, naturally gravitated towards me through a combination of recognition (many would surrender themselves to me with "You look like my aunt" or some other comment that let me know that with me, they felt familiar) and curiosity ("Why would you move from America to live here?" they often would challenge me, looking at me as though I truly had lost my mind that I could ever leave the States and come to Denmark to live). I also experienced how desperate they seemed to be to have role models *who looked like them*. From this experience I have grown to understand how important it is that students see themselves reflected in the staff at their school. Students must see themselves in positions of authority — to not be able to do so is an act of violence.

The kids were mostly born in Denmark. Many spoke at least three languages. They had names like Zanubia, Diab, Hussein, Sumbal and Zeinab, among others. They often travelled to the birthplace of their parents or grandparents only to find out that they were considered Danish, even if some in Denmark did not see them as such. They lived in Denmark and found out they were foreigners here as well. They came from Vesterbro, Blågårds Plads, Nordvest or Ishøj, among other places around the city. Some read thick books while others marvelled at their phones. Some listened to Arabic pop while others took Tupac on as a new religion. I was respected by their parents and felt their support 100%. They all wanted what most of us want for our children: a fighting chance at success here. Some students set their hearts elsewhere, in the US, London, the Netherlands maybe. Countries that had already woven a more successful immigration narrative and promised to offer some relief from what could sometimes be vitriolic attacks by the media or politicians, on immigrants, refugees and asylum seekers.

I bring up my high-school experience because I know

what Denmark has to gain by becoming more inclusive rather than creating a culture that is truly alienating to those who do not fit the norm. It is true that the US has much to learn in the department of diversity — but it is also true that we have amazing examples of possibility.

Once I bumped into a former student of mine, Jumana. I've had the privilege of teaching her and her two sisters. Her parents migrated here from Iraq, and she and her sisters were all born in Denmark. She told me what a shock it was to leave the school and enter the "real world." She went from being in a sea of diversity, to being the only brown and Muslim girl. She told me that the experience, while challenging, had ended up helping her to fit in more and that it improved her self-esteem. As the only young lady who covers her hair with a scarf she told me how no one would even approach her in the beginning. Luckily for her she is a strong, opinionated young women who is encouraged to debate and speak her mind by her family. She may cover her hair — but this is not synonymous with covering her mouth.

* * *

We often speak of tolerance as if to tolerate something is a good thing. It was not too many years ago that Angela Merkel declared multiculturalism a failure.[1] When I read the headline, my heart sank. It was like reading the gravestone for humanity. Europe obviously is going through an identity crisis — and in this crisis, she risks rearing her fascist head and leaving her best resources behind. Now let me be clear about something — I would not call myself a globalist, either. Globalism as I understand it is a corporate capitalist construct — a combination that could never be healthy for anyone. What I do envision, however, is a space where people exercise mutual comprehensions. More on that in a minute.

I say we need to open up our hearts and eyes to the case at hand here in Denmark. There is an entire population that, although it is part of the bigger picture, seems to be left out. This only creates isolation and alienation — something a small country like Denmark needn't embrace. I'm not sure when Denmark made the shift from being an open country to a xenophobic one, but the shift has been made. What to do? Politicians bemoan the whole idea of "parallel societies" here in Denmark, but little attention is given to how policies in housing, employment and education still contribute to isolationism, added to the normalisation of hate speech.

No man or country is an island, and in Denmark where asylum and deportation centres have been accused of inspiring hopelessness and death, I hope something gives, soon. Stories abound of rampant crime, rape (of children as well as adults), isolation and the fact that these centres create a sort of limbo — where occupants are encouraged through deplorable conditions to either voluntarily return to their countries of origin (many don't even have this option) or to die a slow death. As I complete these letters to you, there are currently twenty-eight asylum seekers on hunger strike at Kærshovedgård Departure Centre in protest of conditions there. I have never been to a departure centre (nor a deportation centre) but I have been to an asylum centre, and was surprised to see barbed wiring and limited access and exit points. There are children there. This is a modern tragedy, and one that is destined to grow even worse if we do not come together and understand the *why* of these migrations and how, on a more humane level, to better address them.

Thankfully, there is a community of devoted activists, people who refuse to allow their humanity to be petrified. People like Tone Olaf Nielsen, co-founder and director at

CAMP (Centre for Art on Migration Politics) and co-founder of Trampoline House, which offers integral services to those who need them most and who are often the weakest link in society; Bwalya Sørenson, who started Black Lives Matter here in Denmark and who has successfully linked this movement, originally from the States, to the conditions of African migrants here; Julia Suárez-Krabbe, a professor at Roskilde University whose writing, activism and insistence on critiquing the Eurocentric status quo are refreshing and necessary; the Bridge Radio crew who ensure that voices are heard from this dire situation of exclusion; the Eritrean artist Miriam Firesewra Berhane Haile, whose filmmaking and work promote inclusivity in representation and ensure that we learn about the countries and Western involvement in East Africa; the performance artist and activist Yong Sun Gullach, whose performances and work with the Adoption Political Forum, sheds light on the connections between trans-national adoption and colonialism. Through their work, and that of countless others, they campaign tirelessly for those who have been deemed through policy less free in this democracy.

Integral to white expansionism and capital development is the concentration camp: whether to limit the movements of Black and brown people who flee environmental disasters, occupation or war. Plantations, which became the backbone of European capital, were nothing more than concentration camps; just like so-called Indian reservations or the migrant camps dotting the US, Australia and Europe. Prisons too, especially in the US, serve this purpose as well. The European asylum centre can be added to this. Never forget that the European concentration camps were inspired by the American government's treatment of Native Americans.

* * *

Instead of speaking about tolerance, why don't we adapt the concept of mutual comprehension? The idea of mutual comprehension can be traced back to Simón Bolívar, that South American revolutionary after whom Bolivia is named but who was originally born in Venezuela, a country you can see from Trinidad. He was the individual behind bringing independence from Spain. Simón Bolívar promoted the idea of mutual comprehension, something he had learned from his African nanny. The idea was that through a genuine understanding of each other, unity is forged. To paraphrase a Native American proverb, "Before you criticise a woman, walk a mile in her shoes." So why don't we, in the so-called West, see that it is we who are destroying the world and that our unchecked materialism is responsible for the continual raping of the land and her people? Why don't we embrace the idea that bullying is happening on a large social scale — and that Denmark is, actually, much better than that?

Imagine a student body where the majority of the students speak at least three languages. Imagine a student body who felt empowered and that they belonged, that they were appreciated along with all the other children of Denmark. Imagine them growing up in a country where they truly did believe that there was a chance for success here. Imagine this Denmark, because it is only through our imagining it that we can bring it to reality. Son, I truly hope that the future for all of us includes less tolerance, but more of a mutual comprehension of each other.

On Baldwin

Please try to remember that what they believe, as well as what they do and cause you to endure does not testify to your inferiority but to their inhumanity.
— James Baldwin, *The Fire Next Time*

Dear Son,

When Raoul Peck's 2016 award-winning documentary about James Baldwin, *I Am Not Your Negro*, first screened in Denmark, a group of activists got together and alerted the organisers that they felt such an occasion would benefit from inviting someone who could contextualise the film for a Danish audience. Bwalya Sørensen was among those who recommended me. This is what I read, although I've edited it with you as a reader in mind:

I first met the work of Baldwin when I was twelve years old and living in the small twin-island nation in the Caribbean, Trinidad and Tobago. An avid reader, I was looking through my Uncle John's books when I stumbled across a worn paperback of *If Beale Street Could Talk*. The story takes place in Harlem in the 1970s and chronicles the love between Fonny and Tish, and how that love is challenged when Fonny is falsely accused of rape.

I'll never forget the feeling that overcame me as I read the book under the hot Caribbean sun. I had moved to Trinidad from Brooklyn only about a year or two before, and the world of which he wrote was familiar to me. In fact, just a few years before, I had written a short story in Brooklyn — I was just ten — about a young couple who learned that the main female character was pregnant. In Brooklyn, tales of teenage pregnancy were not uncommon, told to instil fear in the minds of young girls about the consequences of sex. When I flipped to the back of the book and saw his iconic face I immediately set off to learn more about this man.

As he did for so many others, through his work Baldwin became my mentor, my friend, my mother, my father. He was my go-to guide in life and my comfort. He helped me navigate the slippery slope of questioning my religion, Christianity; and put words and order to the world I had been born into. For too many of us whose lives have been damaged by the ravages of European colonialism and the enslavement of our ancestors, there was a need for humanitarian heroes, a hunger for those who look the devil in the eyes and proclaim, loudly, eloquently, "You are indeed a monster." What resonated most profoundly for me and many others about Baldwin was that he'd managed to leave the United States of America to live abroad, gaining a completely different vantage point of America as well as American Blackness. Wrapped up in this migration is a hope that many Blacks harbour — that of escaping white American racism. Further reading of any of his over twenty books and countless essays taught us, his starving young fan base, that the peace that is longed to be experienced in Europe is all too easily punctured. He taught us about the colonial relationship of France towards Algeria and reminded us, lest we forget, that Europe is indeed the birthplace of racism.

When I was a young publishing professional in New York during the Nineties, every other Black writer I came across had pretty much the same experience with Baldwin. Although he wrote in a period decades before our existence, we found the topics that he touched upon still painfully relevant: racism and white America's inability to confront it. Baldwin spoke about difficult subjects in a beautiful language. He was a Black, gay man — and not ashamed of it. In fact, he saw his homosexuality as an integral component of his art and political and social message. These things were not separate for him. His 1956 novel, *Giovanni's Room*, was ground-breaking in that Baldwin not only put homosexuality at the centre of the novel, but interestingly took Blackness out: the main characters in this novel are white. When we think about the power of representation it is important to point out this crucial fact when reviewing his work. Baldwin is a pioneer in speaking truth to power, regarding not just race, but also the lived experiences of what it means to be gay. For a Black man to write a novel with a homosexual protagonist and no major Black characters in the late Fifties was indeed radical. It was a subversive usurpation of power. It is perhaps this novel that endears me the most to him; if just for the very fact that he demonstrates his own literary power and takes me to a place I would otherwise have never come to know. This is the power of art and literature.

No matter what work of Baldwin's you pick up, you will experience the passion and the fury from which he writes. What is indeed most saddening to me is how relevant his work is, still. One of the world's best-kept secrets is that in the United States, freedom has yet to come to the descendants of enslaved Africans. This you learn well even if you do not want to learn it. You learn that segregation continues, under a different language, a different guise. As you get older, if you are privileged enough to travel, you'll learn that the vast majority of neighbourhoods in the US are still, mostly, exclusively white. You'll see whose lives are valued and whose lives are not, whose lives matter — this information is now brought straight into our homes via social media and videos of assassinations of our men, women and children. However, son, I want to make clear that freedom is not possible under capitalism, for anyone. For the cogs of the capitalist machine are well-oiled by the death, labour and blood of Black and brown bodies.

Through Baldwin, you learn about what it means to be gay *and* Black, that some would prefer your existence to be invisible and that there is little protection for your life. You will learn that the woman who accused Emmett Till, the fourteen-year-old who was brutally lynched in Mississippi in 1955, just a year before *Giovanni's Room* was published, admitted to lying about the whole case and that she is still alive and free, as well as the fact that his murderers were never convicted. It was this dead Black boy's body that sparked the Civil Rights Movement.

Despite being in the midst of the UN's International Decade for People of African Descent (2015–24), Western media continues to show people of African descent in an unflattering light. The imagery can be harsh when we talk about diaspora Blacks, whether in rubber boats in the Mediterranean or arriving via international airports. Whiteness will always attempt to wield its control over us, otherwise it will be devoid of power. Whiteness's power is in its lack of empathy and unflinching ability to elicit violence on others. It doesn't even matter if you are a world-renowned writer; in Denmark, you can still be mistaken for a sex worker, as happened to the Nigerian writer Chimamanda Ngozi Adichie on her visit to this country.

* * *

I know it feels like there is not much to give hope these days, but know that I speak to you as a Black woman, who chose to leave the brutality of white racism in the United States of America for a softer, blunter, but no less damaging experience of racism here in Europe. My only wish is that Europe reckons with the dilemmas of race that her ancestors have struggled with and which are now our inheritance. Where we go now is entirely up to how *Europe* does this.

The Road to Hossein

Son,

It is a sunny day in Copenhagen when Hossein texts me this poem:

> We don't know
> Ourselves. We just
> Look like our selves.

He often translates Iranian poems and texts them to his friends when he has had too much red wine to drink. Hossein is depressed, which is not good news for me. See, I've been depressed too, in what has been heralded, too many years in a row, the happiest country in the world. Hossein is sixty years old and it doesn't give me too much relief to see him still struggling in his adopted country of residence.

I tell him to meet me in Christiania, the area in Copenhagen that declared itself a free state back when I was a baby still wearing diapers in Brooklyn. Back then, a group of intrepid souls decided to squat an old military base, and where there once was the staccato roar of military drills, there is now the relatively unhindered sale of hashish and weed. I like the diverse crowd that Christiania attracts. I like the multitude of difference and it is not unusual to sit at the Moonfisher, one of its most popular cafés, and spot senior citizens, squares and alternatives passing time drinking coffee and smoking joints. I often go there to escape the alienation I tend to feel living here in Denmark, gaining much comfort and relief there. There is so much more to Christiania than the sale of hash — there is a forest where one can walk and find solitude in nature.

It is June. The weather has long begun to thaw from the rigid, asphyxiating cold and darkness of Copenhagen winter. Slowly everything has begun to come alive as the palette of vibrant colours unleashed by the changing of the season; colours that together conjure the word "verdant" are now on display. Buds, timid at first, burst upon the scene in a colourful, dynamic blast that heralds the city's awakening. It reminds me of a congregation of Black women in their Sunday best, spilling out of church on a Sunday afternoon in Brooklyn. Birds sing, and with the coming of the sun and the much longer and more colourful days, our hearts have begun to soften toward one another. The natives become relaxed, smiling more and revealing their solar-deprived Nordic bodies unabashedly to the sun like worshippers of the past.

In this awakening I too am feeling a bit livelier, a rambunctiousness welling up from within. With the advent of spring I feel hopeful again. The small leaves that sprout from once barren limbs remind me of my own possibility. *Maybe there is a place for me here in Denmark, after all.*

I ride past the playground where the neighbourhood children play what the entire world refers to as football. I know these kids. I have been seeing them since I moved into this neighbourhood four years ago. They are a colourful mix whose parents are from Somalia, Palestine, Pakistan and Turkey. Today there are two girls on the basketball court-turned-football pitch who run its expanse undeterred by long skirts and headscarves, appearing as graceful as a pair of sailboats on an open sea.

Many of the streets bear names of countries, and I make a left turn off of Norway and onto Holland. Green spills forth from cracks in the concrete, and there is bird chatter incessantly above our heads. There is witchcraft in some of the small gardens I see. Elderberry trees are coming to life; it is a wood once thought magical by the ancestors of the people whose land I now inhabit.

I bike through my neighbourhood, Amager. The locals still refer to it as "shit island" because it was once used as an area for garbage disposal in the 1970s, but Amager is no longer the dumping ground for the city's garbage (although some would beg to differ). Now, like many other Copenhagen neighbourhoods, it is thriving. There seems to be a café of some kind or another on every corner, and whenever I get homesick the local mall lulls me into believing that I landed in some alternate-universe United States suburban experiment where the inhabitants speak an undecipherable English.

The demographic landscape of Amager is under transformation. It is like this all over Copenhagen — metro stations being installed in every likely cultural and commercial hub in town, with pneumatic drills piercing and penetrating the earth below so that new buildings can grow from the earth, so eager to perform. Property value is going up and construction is non-stop.

Amager has its charm despite what its neighbours think. When I think about it I see it has the same relationship that Manhattanites once displayed — or perhaps in their psychosis still do — toward Brooklyn. It is really just snobbery that imagines, *based on location*, one group of people to be inferior to another. It is the same attitude that those in Copenhagen share for their fellow Jutlanders; that unfortunate soul to be born on the mainland as opposed to on *the devil's island*, as the island Copenhagen is sometimes referred to by the mainlanders. Do you know why there is water surrounding Zealand (the island that Copenhagen is on)? Because, according to those in Jutland, *it was too expensive to erect a fence.*

I bike down Amagerbrogade, past the various shops that adorn this stretch offering shoes, ice-cream, espresso, world-famous Danish pastries, breads, health foods and wine. I go across the road that separates my neighbourhood from the now elite neighbourhood of Christianshavn. It is not unusual to pass a native of Christianshavn lamenting the colonisation of their neighbourhood by new money that is driving up rents and rendering it impossible for the children of the original residents to continue any lineage there. Christianshavn was built as a fortification for Copenhagen in the seventeenth century. There is a metro stop and a bevy of stores and shops to keep its inhabitants content. It is also known as Little Amsterdam. There are canals that reflect the small, quaint yellow- and mauve-painted houses. This is home to the original Layer Cake House — an institution of sorts, whose pastries and cakes are one of this country's specialties. The variety of breads on display resemble sumptuous cartoonish bricks, many of them grainy and jam-packed with seeds. There are the usual regalia of French flutes, croissants and rugbrød (a grainy, dark bread). Then there are the selection of cakes and pastries that glitter like precious gems in the showcases. But as noted in my previous letter to you, this building once imprisoned rebellious women, including Queen Marie, who sought to cleanse the evils of racism and capitalism with fire.

I remember that one morning I went to the Lagerkagehus, and as I stood in line I noticed a girl of about nine years ogling me. Having been here for seventeen years, I've gotten used to kids checking me out. This particular little girl was doing that thing kids do where they try to look like they're talking to the adults they are with, but the direction of their gaze — their eyes — gives them away. She was brown-haired with grey eyes, and her t-shirt was too small for her little round belly, so her navel peeked out like a winking eye. Her pants were too tight for a kid and soon she started looking to me a bit like an elf and I couldn't take it anymore. I broke through her stare and asked her where she was from.

She told me she was from Brooklyn! Meanwhile her accompanying adult let me know through her own glance of suspicion that she was not feeling me. Moments like these make me wish I knew how to get some kind of extra spiritual body protection from *the draft* — that racist glare that Art Blakey so eloquently referred to whenever he felt he was about to perform before a racist crowd. I feel a draft, he'd let his bandmates know. And sometimes I do feel like I need the supernatural in order to survive *the glare*.

I told them that I'm also from Brooklyn. At the declaration of this tiny bit of common information the woman's eyes immediately melted, and she stepped forward in a reconciliatory manner. She told me where exactly they are from in *our* Brooklyn. I'm not sure why she was looking at me so suspiciously before, and there is even a chance she was unaware of her initial posture, but she eased next to me like we were long-lost best friends. I bought my bread and walked out, wondering why telling people I'm from Brooklyn or New York usually elicits a response akin to celebrity. Experiences such as this merely solidify my awareness of the romantic ideas many here have of New York, fed to them through Woody Allen films and Paul Auster books. It is not that I think this is a terribly wrong phenomenon — it is just that I find it naïve and gullible.

* * *

As I ride along on my way to Hossein I see the little bistros filled with young professionals dressed in Scandinavian-styled black and grey, intoxicated with the feeling that recently acquired material success imbues. Word has it that there has been a recession for some time, although aside from the growing wave of bottle collectors and homelessness it is difficult to fathom judging solely from the look of many locals. I am told, however, that Denmark has the world's fourth-largest personal debt, although ranking only sixth in terms of world salaries. Not sure how that will unravel. The reality of that fact looms like a harbinger akin to the cold dark winters here in Copenhagen, and I catch myself wondering how it will play itself out in the future. Recently, Denmark has been offering loans with *negative* interest.

I take the scenic route into Christiania on my way to meet Hossein rather than via its main entrance on Princess Street, a path often packed with people coming and going. There's a roasted-peanut vendor there and during the warmer months many hang out in the sidewalks right outside. I ride past the sign that reads, "You are now leaving the EU and entering the free state of Christiania." To avoid the crowd of tourists — and the police — I make a right onto the back road.

The bodies of water that surround this area give it a fairy-tale feeling that conjures up Hans Christian Andersen tales. And if you are familiar at all with his stories as well as Christiania, then you know I do not necessarily mean to conjure enchantment. There is something brutal, too, in Hans Christian Andersen's work — trauma-inducing worlds where the prose is beautiful and the stories haunting — something embedded that is fatal, perhaps, to one's spirit. Tales that continue the tradition of instilling fear, so that behaviours can be controlled, with lessons full of regret, loss and brutality.

Although many people like to use the term "fairy tale" when they visit wonderful Copenhagen, it ought to be noted that the fairy tales that are most often referred to were created by this odd man who was a failed ballet dancer. Andersen, as most may not know, made his living as a playwright and it is here that my interest swells: for amongst the many plays he wrote for the Danish aristocracy there is one entitled *Mulat* that every Dane should be required to read. To resurrect this side of Andersen will indeed awake even the sleepiest of Danes to their colonial history, a history that has been pushed to the margins, denied and whitewashed. Luckily for us there are artists here, such as Trinidadian Danish artist Jeannette Ehlers, who bring works such as this into the present, allowing us to contemplate these works in the now.

I cannot deny that it fills me with happiness that there is so much nature — even in the centre of the city. This is one of the reasons I decided to stay here. In Copenhagen, it is possible to see sky, unobstructed. But I do remain mindful of shadows.

I bike on the asphalt and the smell of grilled green peppers and sausages envelopes me.

The trees that surround the moat of Christiana are beech, oak and ash. And the smooth asphalt turning into dirt and gravel signal that I have officially entered the free state. The eclectic mix of do-it-yourself houses that occupy this former military base are also a good hint that one is there. The houses all bear signs of home repair, with some residents even installing solar panels. There is an elaborate sculpture made with rustic materials like wood and rocks. Christiania — technically a squat — has only a few hundred inhabitants, and I am curious how the continuation of this free state will fare under the changing times of our world.

As we all know here, Christiania's relationship with the Danish state is also quite tenuous. Because it boasts itself as a "free state," there is the sale of hashish in the open market. However, this is against the laws of the Danish state: and it is this particular issue that many observe rather excitedly, to see how this will unfold. I don't like it when the Danish police, replete with riot and anti-terrorism gear, swarm down Pusher Street, with the pushers fighting back with masked faces, smoke bombs and angry words. Lately, this seems to be a thing of the past since the inhabitants of Christiania decided to kick out the hash dealers from Pusher Street, creating, once again, a more relaxed atmosphere in this free state.

I make a left onto the little wooden bridge that takes me across the moat and I see birds preparing for the continuation of the cycle of their existence, and the tableau feels a bit like something from a storybook. Or as if it has inspired one at least. Mute swans, protected by the crown, are ushering their young into the world. The wise never walk too near to them and their hiss is usually enough to secure their space both on land and water. I remember that once, when you were little, you asked about the swans and their cygnets, you asked why they were not white like their parents. I answered that it was because they were babies, to which you responded, "Do you mean that when I grow up, I'll be white too?"

People sit all along the body of water on both sides, and green beer bottles reflect the glare of the sun as they are lifted to lips after the perfunctory *skål* (cheers), which supposedly means "skull" because, as some incorrectly say, that was what the Vikings drank out of. Beer here is omnipotent. Even in the neighbourhood of Vesterbro, the Carlsberg sign looms above like the neighbourhood's own, private moon.

I pull up to the Moonfisher and it is teeming with folks who have allowed their usual orderliness and stoicism to melt with the coming of the sun.

I see familiar faces. There is Andrew, the African Celt from Manchester. And Linda, the American writer who has just completed her novel about this very same place. There is Line, the Queen of the Underground, whose huge apartment is jam-packed with taxidermied, dead animals and antique sewing machines. The whole area is alive and the smell of hashish permeates the air. Conversations range from Denmark's political relationship to the US to sports and of course aliens.

I spot Hossein sitting against the white wall and walk over and take a seat next to him. Hossein tells me that his wife of over thirty years has decided to leave him. It is not comforting to me that my older friends still suffer from issues of the heart. To be completely honest, and I know I am being selfish here, I wish he were not here, at sixty years of age, lamenting a failed relationship. I want to say to him, "You are not supposed to be having these kind of relationship problems at your age! If this is the case... there is no hope for me!" But I am old enough now to know that no matter how old you are, life happens.

Hossein is originally from Iran. A son of a lower military official, he was not rich, but he was also certainly not poor. Like so many of his generation in Iran, education became the new religion. A possible ticket into the world of so-called meritocracy. A path to a better life. He managed to study his way from a primary school built on a cemetery (where he has told me of a classmate who once gnawed on human bones in exchange for pennies) to university.

Hossein was "lucky" to get a job in Turkey teaching English, not too long after the "Iranian Revolution" — the moment when Iran, once so potent with promise and hope, found itself hijacked by a US-sponsored religious cleric. But Hossein was clever and managed to escape. Life, he thought, with his young Persian wife and son at his side, held promise.

Until you speak to political refugees here in Denmark, stories of expatriation to Denmark tend to be dull. They run the rather mundane gamut of love, or what my British friend Jane once quipped was "the Danish gene-pool project." According to her, this project is an age-old ploy that has been used throughout the centuries to spice up Danish genetics (lest things get a little too royal around here).

Sometimes I think to myself that she does have a bit of a point, inasmuch as I can't help but notice, much to my chagrin, how biracial children seem to be sometimes exotified here. I wonder how or if this has impacted you? My hope is that you do not grow up as I have noticed some other biracial Danes here do: thinking that they are better than others. As each generation sprouts its virginal head in Copenhagen, it is the *mulat* — as biracial offspring are so stubbornly referred to here in Denmark — whose melanin shines like gold on skin, who seem to be oft coveted. Despite the fact that the term *mulatto* refers to mules and is in fact a description borne from plantocracy, some Blacks *and* whites insist on using the word. Do you remember that time we were on the train coming back from Berlin and a young lady, a model, insisted on speaking to you to hear of your interest in modelling? "They love your type!" she said, much too loudly for our comfort!

"Oh, don't be so sensitive," is the usual response when you attempt to get many to show a little historical wisdom. "What's all this about being politically correct? You people need to get a sense of humour! You're not going to make us like Sweden!" This usually follows some rendition of Blackface or insult to a people's religion. To be fair, there are many Danes who do not fit this bill. But unfortunately, they don't seem to be the ones who are controlling the media, or at least have influence over any kind of meaningful cultural change.

I haven't failed to see that Copenhagen is peppered with caramel-coloured kids who spend the first part of their lives upset that their parents broke social taboos (or played into them), thereby making their offspring different; and then the other half exploiting the clumsy genius inherent in being interracial. They too, however, will soon realise that in Denmark, no one is special.

Expats are also cajoled here by foreign corporate hire — whether they are private or state. Families are lured by exorbitant tax-free salaries, so that if chosen, there need only be one breadwinner in the family. Mostly, it's the men who command these high salaries, with the wives, usually just as educated if not more so, receiving the luxury of being able to stay at home navigating motherhood in a foreign country. They are the ones who must negotiate this foreign terrain — grocery stores full of foreign-labelled products that hammer in the distance from home. They are the ones who have to figure out how to say "flour" in Danish (*mel*); to make appointments with the variety of state agencies that seem to demand it; and to find such fine American products like Oreo cookies and Betty Crocker cake mix. Many of these episodes occur in Hellerup, although not exclusively. These women learn quickly through folding themselves into tight networks how to secure a turkey for Thanksgiving, and that in Denmark you pay for your plastic shopping bags. Many of these families will be visited by some sort of medication-induced calm at some point, and perhaps suffer from an extreme case of xenophobia where Denmark becomes the root of all evil, and one can find oneself spiralling head-first into a depression that sticks to the bones like congealed Crisco and weighs heavily on the soul. Don't get me wrong, one's existence here needn't be so bleak: the natives, as you know all too well, do promote alcoholism, which usually pops you over really good, until you're done!

None of these tales, however, are the ones that can claim Hossein. He left Iran intent on returning. He saw the life of a cultivated intellectual as his for the taking. He read Persian poetry in the moonlight and enjoyed the freedom of red wine. He was a progressive at heart and took pride that he could reconfigure the world through a myriad of literary references, most of them Western, some of them Persian, and none Arabic.

But there was something amiss in Turkey. It is illegal to demonstrate against the government there. Although Hossein had other things to do, it soon became apparent that at least one of his students did not. And unfortunately for Hossein, when a man is arrested in Turkey, so is his phone book.

This was a time when Danes could travel the world with their flags proudly sewn on their backpacks as though they were Canadians, when Danes felt their government was standing up for something, and there was still everyday mundane merchandise, such as t-shirts, made in Denmark. This was a time when Danes could protest in the street relatively unhindered as though it was their *right*. It was the time before the demonstrations against the Maastricht Treaty, in which the police would shoot bullets into the crowd, hurting at least four, and before they rounded up and arrested activists even before they stepped into Denmark, as they did for the G8 conference in 2009. All of this quite legal apparently, due to anti-terror laws.

It was in this great tradition of Danish activism that a group of Danish activists made it their responsibility to get Hossein out of Turkish prison. The hitch? He would have to move to Denmark. This is the part of the story where Hossein, when repeating it, breaks out in hysterical laughter. You know the kind — where your eyes begin to tear up and your emotions get confused about whether it is extreme joy you are experiencing, or the pain inherent in occupying the absolute depths of despair.

People are really happy here. Life here is good. The standard of living is high... but no one seems to mention the high suicide rate — one of the highest in the world at *four* people per day. Or the high rate of happy pills that are dispensed at the mention of a headache. No one talks about the high level of alcoholism. And when you do? "Don't be so negative!" comes the reply.

Yes, it is true the sun shines on Denmark — sometimes.

I ask Hossein if he thinks he's depressed. "Depressed?" he asks, "Oh, Lesley, don't sound so American."

* * *

I know Hossein is lonely.

I have a friend back in New York named Reggie, originally from the Bronx but who now lives in London. Reggie is a gentleman with a dramatic flair about him. My flamingo-pink sequinned hot-pants were inherited from him once he decided to move on to something with a bit more flair. Reggie insists the best therapy for depression is boxes of cheap dinnerware from tacky discount chain stores. He attributes his actual survival to the existence of cheap dinner plates created, his imagination has assured him, with the distinct purpose of allowing modern humans to express through them deep grief, disappointment, anger and fury.

In listening to Reggie tell his story and actually picturing him in my own head acting out his therapeutic rationale, I am sure this is how he survived the intensely cut-throat NYC Black gay scene of the 1990s.

Reggie would walk right into a discount store, the kind where everything is priced at ninety-nine cents, with no less presence or stature than the East Side elite who waltz into Bergdorf's or Saks Fifth Avenue. He'd go over to the housewares department and pick up a box of the always-50%-off dinnerware. Nothing too fancy — just earthenware surface area. I imagine him wearing oversized Jackie O sunglasses, a V-neck t-shirt that feels like silk to the touch, and his signature size-twenty-eight Jordache jeans. He'd pay for the box of plates and continue to his East Village apartment, looking like a caricature of the scale of Justice… a tiny Marc Jacobs bag dangling from one wrist, and the much larger one full of his dinnerware, dangling from the other, both bags equally necessary for the form of balance in his mind. When he reached his apartment building, instead of opening his own front door, he'd continue ceremoniously up the stairs to the rooftop. There, he would unpack the box. Gently. He would remove and unwrap each item, and after a moment of careful study to reflect on how the word China has been reduced to mass produced cobalt blue and lacquer dinnerware, Reggie would methodically toss each plate from the roof of his building. The awaiting asphalt of the Lower East Side has seen much worse. Pieces of shattering white plates, as they formed starbursts, would be a relief for Reggie. Release. A freedom of sorts. From all the anguish. From all the bullshit. Just for a little while. Unsuspecting passers-by would look up. And then they keep moving, even less shocked than the asphalt. Unsuspecting passers-by are only unsuspecting until they recognise the pattern. This is New York. There are more unusual things in the streets of New York than pieces of broken dinnerware. On the Lower East Side, had they known Reggie — had they been aware of his plans — the audience of humans may very well have joined him. The police, back then, were never called. Reggie, thusly, in specific moments of his own constructed theatre, expressed to the universe his pain. Discount dinner plates at the ninety-nine-cent stores are still for sale.

* * *

I think of this memory of Reggie and I look at Hossein. I realise that Hossein is slowly having a breakdown. It's like slow motion because there is no space for him to just safely fall apart. But if there is no space for a breakdown, how can we break through and become whole again, healthy?

When you were younger you'd say to me every Sunday, "We're back on the hamster wheel tomorrow."

Is it just me — or does time accelerate and sometimes slow down without ever really moving at all?

You say to me, "Mom, I don't want to go to school. School is boring." Who are you telling?

* * *

I used to work at the same school Hossein ended up working in after Denmark saved him from a Turkish prison. Hossein has been there for fourteen years. I've since left and now teach adults. Hossein, however, is no longer a teacher. Coming to Denmark changed that. Coming to Denmark somehow imprinted on him the idea that he could not fulfil his dreams. Instead, Hossein, still reciting and translating poetry only when drunk, has found himself a kind of *altmuligmand* — doing a little bit of this and that at the school. I call it the *immigrant syndrome*: that of taking jobs you are clearly over-qualified for.

I wonder if I should buy Hossein and myself cheap dinnerware?

* * *

Hossein is an artist. And when I say artist, I implore you to reclaim the meaning inherent in the word as our human right. *To create is to exalt life, no?* So said a Catalan guitar-playing landscape artist I once met in this free-state-within-a-state of Christiania, which intermittently receives threats of reclamation from the Danish state. To be fair, there's nothing smart about starting a free state within a country trying to catch up with the cool kids in the cafeteria, and even less smart that you do so on what is obviously prime real estate. It's a challenge to be different in a country like Denmark, where rules and social cues are engraved in stone and its citizens are quick to police each other. Try crossing the street on a red light and soon enough some non-descript

Danish person will yell at you, more upset that you have broken the law than the fact that you may have risked your life.

Denmark sometimes can feel like a place where dreams go to die. Remember the Law of Jante: you're not special, you're not as good as we are, you're not smarter than us, you're not better than us, you're not more important, you're not good at anything, you can't laugh at us, YOU can't teach us anything!

It's been years now since Hossein's wife left him. Since then he has given up drinking and has even returned to Iran a couple of times after discovering that he would not be under any threat. He had been terrified to go before, so terrified that he didn't even risk returning on the death of his parents. But last year, he returned. Iran has changed much since he left, he told me. And as I look at my friend Hossein, I reply, and so have you, my dear friend. And so have you.

The life of exile, my dear son, cannot be an easy one. And while I sometimes speak of my presence here as some sort of exile, let us remember it is a self-imposed one and I have always, although I haven't always acted upon it, been able to go back to the States. I often wonder about all my fellow human beings around the planet, for whom home remains a distant, far-away vision, only to be visited through fading photographs and memories, if that. I wonder about the amazing women I have met here from Eritrea, Somalia, Iran, Iraq, Afghanistan, Yemen, Palestine, Syria — who have been displaced or murdered because of illegal wars and/or occupation, which in the end only leaves the sober-minded to wonder: what is terrorism?

The Lion Learns to Write: A Visit to My Brother in Jail

Son,

Do you know how to breathe?

Sometimes I catch myself breathing shallow breaths from my chest. The kind of breaths that if I'm not careful could trigger hyperventilation. It could be while I'm shopping in fluorescent-lit grocery stores that offer plastic-covered vegetables and an array of products that tend to leave me dizzy in confusion (there is just so much there!) or it could be in the middle of teaching. *I can't breathe* is what I hear in my mind whenever I catch myself being complicit in my own demise. Whenever I forget to balance an inhale, all the way down to my navel, allowing the oxygen to nourish my blood only to be pushed out again, expelling that which my body cannot use. *I can't breathe* is what I hear myself saying, in my mind, whenever I catch myself amid short, panic-induced breaths as I feel the cortisone coursing through my body. My heart accelerates, my body is in flight mode: this is what I feel when I feel anxiety.

Do you know how to breathe, son? *Never forget to breathe, in through your nose, all the way down to your navel, expand your stomach: and then allowing your navel to reach back into your spine, release through your mouth.*

Being in nature helps me with this.

* * *

I went out for a run this morning. I ran from our apartment over to Langelinie — it was early in the morning and so I had the empty Copenhagen streets all to myself. I ran past the Little Mermaid and along the harbour where the opera house could be seen. *Copenhagen is so beautiful.*

I spoke to your Aunt Shelley yesterday — and she told me about your grandmother's recent visit. Your grandmother, like the rest of us, is getting old and I do so worry about her.

Like me, your Grandma Beryl moved to another country to make it her home. Like me, she gave birth to a child in a place other than her own birthplace. Grandma Beryl has lived in New York for almost fifty years and she proudly holds on to her Trinidadian accent like a badge of honour (which I understand because it is so beautiful). Sometimes you can hear an almost imperceptible African American twang that has snuck in, claiming a part of her voice.

Why would a woman give birth to her child in a foreign country?

* * *

I can't breathe is the phrase that launched over fifty demonstrations across the US when Eric Garner was murdered by a police officer on July 2014 in Staten Island, a borough not too far from where I was born.

I can't breathe.

In New York, hate crimes have gone up by 100% since 45 has been installed, a trend that has many concerned. In America, white nationalists march in Virginia screaming, "white lives matter." This in addition to the fact that our government contains known white supremacists, some even working closely with 45. Add to this the fact that immediately after 45's inauguration, the largest union of police in the US made sure to hand in a special request to *remove the ban on racial profiling*. And, not least, the FBI has introduced a new terrorist threat level, "Black Identity Extremists," which, before it was created, did not seem to exist.

People always ask me why I moved to Denmark — especially when they hear that I am from New York — and often this question is full of disbelief. I have stopped attempting to answer this question and now simply reply, "It's really not dinner-table conversation." For me, there is not just one reason why I moved here. There are a variety of reasons: it is the birthplace of your father; I had always envisioned myself living abroad; there are things I love about Denmark; and, well, in the US *I felt like I could not breathe.*

The last time I visited New York a young man had just been shot at the bodega right around the corner from where I was staying. I was reminded of this every day when I walked down St Nicholas in Harlem by the flowers and candles that were placed for him on the site where he lost his life.

Gun violence is something that I grew up with, and it was something that I did not want you to grow up with. Danes often express disbelief at the US's fascination with guns, forgetting the violence that white settler colonisation is premised upon.

Once, when I was thirteen, there was a shoot-out at a basement party in Brooklyn. The only two people to get shot were my brother's girlfriend and her friend, Imani. They survived, but I'll never forget the panic that spread throughout the crowd, and how we fled out of the basement, me into an apartment building, and into to a stranger's apartment, frightened for my life. I'll never forget finally getting the nerve to leave the apartment, the kindness of the stranger who allowed me to stay there, and as I walked back out into the Brooklyn street, seeing an ambulance and hearing my friend India's voice call me, "Lesley! Shannon got shot!"

There's the senseless death that you must get used to, of friends losing their lives over something as stupid as a parking place (rest in peace Gerard) or having metal detectors installed in your New York City high school, years before 9/11 and airports began to the do the same. Social control often starts in Black communities.

There's the time when a police officer pulled a gun on me and proceeded to force me to walk six blocks to the precinct, with the loaded firearm pointed at my back, in full view of an otherwise normal West Village day in New York City. That was the day I realised that no matter what my accomplishments, nothing could ever protect me from the racism of America. It was weird too because when I was younger, like many others, I experimented with clothes a lot. Some days I looked really girlie and had what we called the "village" look — artsy and chill. But there were some days where I really just felt comfortable in baggy jeans, big t-shirts, construction boots and a huge bomber jacket — which is what a lot of girls from the boroughs wore. I was dressed this way on the day the police almost killed me.

I often wonder, how do we transcend the border of our skin and the control that the death project attempts? The control is not so obvious here in Denmark — I have an American passport and I do not fear the cops here. I am however aware that if I looked another way and had another passport, or if for some reason I was in the wrong place at the wrong time, my reality would be different. I have heard many stories of women who look like me who get harassed by security guards from private companies on public transportation. The red line here is that they all happen to be refugees. Is this a coincidence?

I am also aware that while I enjoy certain privileges here in Denmark, there are currently many other people here who, because of their nationality, do not have these rights. When we look closely at what is currently being described as a "migrant crisis" in Europe — with thousands of people drowning every year in the Mediterranean alone — it is hard not to see this as a symptom of a failing global economic, political and environmental infrastructure.

With sickness usually comes clarity. There can sometimes be nothing more inspiring than a bout of inactivity, a forced contemplation when your body declares "No more!" and your mind is left to wander, to wonder about the meaning of it all. Perhaps this is why I begin this letter to you now — immediately after a particularly stubborn malaise that has refused to leave me in the darkness of Denmark's winters. As I lay in bed, alternating between the deep sleep of sickness, the internet and the countless books that scatter around my bed like gifts in a shrine, my thoughts come back to you. I turn to writing my thoughts on the page so that I can tease out some sense of *why I am here*.

Why are you here? is a common refrain you hear as an immigrant here. The answer many of us have armed ourselves with is in the words of Stuart Hall: *Because you were there.*

You told me recently that you watched the Netflix documentary *13th* by Ava DuVernay, which shows the connection between slavery and the astronomical imprisonment rate of African Americans in the US. Although countless of Danes travel to the States every year, and Danish society is very much influenced by American culture, there still seems to be very little understanding of what life is truly like for poor Americans.

Having someone you're close to in prison is like having a part of your soul imprisoned somewhere, far away, and you're not sure if you'll ever get it back. In 2015 the *Nation* published an article that estimated a total of 2.7 million children in the US had a parent in prison.[1] My nephew and niece, my brother's two children, were two of them. As you know, your uncle was recently released from prison and my days are so much brighter now. In the United States today we have more people in jail than any other country on earth. And with Attorney General Jeff Sessions, there is no sign that this will become better.

On 15 May 2017, Senator Bernie Sanders wrote in a Facebook post:

> We are spending $80 billion a year to lock up 2.2 million Americans, disproportionately African Americans, Latinos and Native Americans. The number of incarcerated drug offenders has increased twelvefold since 1980. This is expensive and it is a waste of human potential. We must end the over-incarceration of nonviolent Americans who do not pose a serious threat to our society. By directing his federal prosecutors to charge drug crime defendants with the most serious, provable crimes carrying the most severe penalties, Attorney General Jeff Sessions is moving us backwards as a society.[2]

Your Uncle Gerry and Aunt Shelley began their lives in Trinidad. They were both born and raised there for their first decade. While in Trinidad they lived with my grandmother, and then later with my mother's aunt. When they were eleven and twelve years old, respectively, they were sent to live with my mother and father in Brooklyn. The move could not have been easy for two Trinidadian children who were unaccustomed to the big city, cold weather and a moody father. Although I only lived with my sister and brother for a total of about five years, it was long enough for us to develop a relationship with each other. Although we have had many differences, I feel so blessed to have your Aunt Shelley and Uncle Gerry in my life. They have been great older siblings. I remember during the New York City blackout of '77, how I jumped into my older sister's arms from the time the lights went out till they came back on again. Gerry was always my backup whenever I got into any fights in school (there were a lot of those).

I remember, when we were young, Gerry being sent to the store to buy my father something, most probably a Guinness stout. My brother got mugged (he must have only been around twelve). I also remember that our father had forbidden us to use the bathroom because he felt it "disturbed" his musical practice; and how my grandmother fiercely stood up for us and demanded that we be allowed this dignity.

Even though I feared my father, I was the one who spent most time with him, as he took care of me while Shelley and Gerry were in school. Because my sister was older, my father was really strict towards her. It was a fact that at nine years old, I had more freedom than my teenage sister. While I went to Empire skating rink with my friend's mother who took all the kids in the building, my sister would have to stay at home.

There were many times my father got violent when he got angry — he even broke a glass in my sister's face not too long after she arrived from Trinidad to live with them. I remember he'd beat Gerry so badly that he'd have marks on his back and skin. It is not unusual for children to move out early when they grow up in such emotionally unstable homes, and Shelley would eventually run away at sixteen. I'll always remember that she had me throw her bag out of our sixth-floor window and the sound that her can of hairspray made when it tumbled out of her bag and hit the pavement. My brother would leave home when he was seventeen and later I too, although under much different circumstances, would also leave at sixteen.

Your Aunt Shelley gravitated towards the creative energy of Greenwich Village, danced and experimented with Rastafarianism and became a vegetarian. She had a huge poster of Jimi Hendrix over her bed and she was an amazing storyteller, often telling me stories at night to get me to sleep. Gerry built bikes and played soccer. He breakdanced on the street back in the day and would later DJ at some of NYC's biggest clubs, like Mars. He was still a teenager when he became a father. His child's mother was only sixteen when she became pregnant and he was seventeen. Despite this age, there was celebration around his child's impending arrival, because even when in the darkest of tribulations in life, birth manages to conjure this magical feeling of hope, of possibility, of love. Despite their young age, they did seem to love each other in whatever way that we learn to love amidst the tall concrete buildings of Brooklyn. We grab our metaphors from the grass growing between the cracks and the blooming trees that insist amongst pavement.

In writing you this letter I realise now that I must endeavour to slow down — something that does not come easily to me. As the youngest of three in a very particular kind of family, I have been made to feel as though I have come into this world running — as if the ancestors wished for me to be a part of the remedy to fix that which has yet to be reckoned with. But for me to fulfil my purpose, I have had to learn to slow down. I am still learning.

Writing has always been that which has forced me to reflect on my life — the scenes, through writing, are slowed down through the thickness of memory. It's like seeing scenes take place through molasses — that dark and sweet substance that so many lives in the Caribbean were called forth for, were destroyed for, to feed an insatiable market in Europe and other parts of the Americas. Yesterday it was sugar, today it is cobalt.

Although my smarts were recognised from an early age, it did little to soften the impatience some of the women in my family seemed to have for me. Sometimes there is nothing more despised than an abandoned child.

I tell you all this just so you know the environment from which I come, and from which your uncle is also a product. However, our experiences have been different, and I share with you these stories so that you can see the gamut of life experiences that can be found in America.

* * *

You should know that one of the reasons I didn't take you to the States the last time was because I wanted to visit your uncle, my brother, in jail. He had gotten arrested the summer before that, and I wanted to offer him some respite. Son, there is something about incarceration in the way that we practice it in the US that is just not civilised.

I called his son, who I hadn't seen in over ten years. It's important for a family to have a strong matriarch. Without my grandmother, my little family has done our best to be there for each other. However, due to the constraints of money and time, too many of our lives have been lived without the presence of the others. I hope to change this. My brother's son, my nephew, lives in another state than New York, and I offered to fly him in so that he and I could spend some time together on our way to seeing Gerry.

This trip was the first time I had been to New York in over four years — and every time I go back to New York I learn that it is not that easy to come home. The term *root trauma* deals with the loss that many feel when the home of their childhood is no longer there. I first came across the term not that long ago, and it made me think about a conversation I had with a friend of mine recently. Her name is Angela Cruz and she lives in Hawaii. She works with ancestral healing. She talked about our root chakra and its connection to home... A couple of the concepts related to the root chakra are survival and home, and their relationship to one another. We would have to first consider what we perceive as the concept of home. Do we consider home to be solely a physical entity? Or does it go beyond that? In Angela's perception home is so much more than the physical thing that we generally refer to. She explains:

Yes, I know it is a truly wonderful gift to be able to come "home" after a long day or after traveling, and be in an environment that we are comfortable and at peace in. Where we can kick up our feet and relax into our true selves. But what about being able to do that wherever we are in this world? What about being able to find comfort and peace in any environment? Then perhaps that means finding true peace and comfort within ourselves, so that we may be at home within ourselves. That would mean truly searching for internal peace, and not seeking external reflections for what we may think peace and home really is. In relation to survival, once we are at peace in our "home", meaning our own physical, emotional, and spiritual being, then we are no longer striving or scrambling to "survive" in this world. We are now simply living and being. You ask why isn't it our universal birthright. Oh but it is! this is most definitely our universal birthright. We were simply given a task here as humans to rediscover what it is to simply be at "home." And this process of discovery has so many incredible effects. If you become fully at home in yourself, and your root chakra is open and vibrating.[3]

There was nowhere left for me to go other than "home" — whatever that meant at that time in my life, or whatever that means to so many of us who have found their childhood neighbourhoods being invaded by colonisers not that different from those of the past. The poet and urban geographer Teju Adisa-Farrar and I were recently talking about migrations. She told me that migrations, such as what can be seen in the process of gentrification and the more recent waves to Europe, is often reversed every fifty or so years. This means, according to her, that Brooklyn might be ours again.

> With this in mind, urbicide — the deliberate death of the city and wilful place annihilation — can stand in as a viable explanation for the ongoing destruction of a black sense of place in the Americas. Urbicide, which has been defined as "the murder of the city" and the "deliberate denial or killing of the city" […] draws attention to the aforementioned sites of environmental, social, and infrastructural deterioration and geographic surveillance that demarcate many black geographies and their inhabitants. Put differently, urbicide is one sensible conceptual tool that can make sense of the interlocking and connective tenets of place, poverty, and racial violence in the Americas.[4]

My brother and the mother of his child, young and trapped on Herkimer Street, Brooklyn, welcomed and received the birth of their son as an offering of hope. Hope that they could do for him so much that was not done by their parents for them. They, like most others, wanted a better life. And, impatient with the cards that they had been dealt, they did what most other youngsters did: break out of childhood for the promising life of adulthood.

But what was this space that these young parents, still children, found themselves in? Brooklyn, your uncle's friend Terry reminds us, is the borough of Kings. Brooklyn, since its inception in 1683 by the Dutch, has always, like everywhere else in the United States, although certainly more so than other parts of the country, been the place for immigrants. There's dispute as to what Brooklyn really means, with some suggesting that it is broken Dutch for "Broken Land." This is the Brooklyn that your parents, and many more of us, know.

Who was in Brooklyn, before us? I was lucky to have a fourth-grade teacher, Mrs Stein, who spent the whole year teaching her class of mostly Black and brown students about Native American history. She was a Jewish woman and passionate about teaching us about anti-discrimination. With her peroxide-blonde hair and loving approach in her teaching, she ensured that I would never hate white people. It was Mrs Stein who told us about the buffalo, and how it was the Europeans who slaughtered them, in their quest to erase the indigenous people of America, or of what they themselves referred to as Turtle Island.

I could talk about the various groups of other immigrants who made Brooklyn, more accurately Flatbush, home. There are the Jews, the Irish, the Italians, the Poles. The African Americans who moved up north fleeing white terrorism from the south and seeking opportunity, such as Willie-Mae and her own family. The people who were on Turtle Island before the Armageddon of their world, the people who were in the area we know as New York, were called the Lenape. They were a peaceful people who are considered to be the grandfathers of all the other indigenous groups in North America. Did you know that the indigenous people of the Americas have been there for over thirty thousand years?

But perhaps I'm going too fast. Again.

I went back to New York because I needed to come home. I hadn't been to Brooklyn in four years — too long.

"Can I live?" asks Jay-Z in his ground-breaking debut that showcased and refined the hustling-Black-man archetype through hip hop, drug dealing and criminality. Feeding the desperate dreams of countless young boys to grow up in Brooklyn after him, providing the soundtrack for their runs, busts and dreams; hey, it's not Jay-Z's fault that that was the best some neighbourhoods could offer after being supplied with drugs and guns by what some people claim to be the

US government.

I left New York because at some point everyone must ask themselves about the role they are playing in their own demise. I recognised that although we Brooklynites and New Yorkers seem to have an unquestioning and unbreakable bond to New York (no matter how jaded we are we will always light up when Alicia Keys sings out loud), that New York, and Brooklyn by default, had no such loyalty for me.

Add this to the fact that there is really no home left for me in New York. If I go to 1199 Ocean Avenue today, there is only one familiar person left in the building in which I spent my years before being sent to Trinidad. Gone is my mother-in-spirit Willie-Mae and her daughter India who guided me into an empowering Black womanhood, with love, laughter and style.

> About 15 million children in the United States – 21% of all children – live in families with incomes below the federal poverty threshold, a measurement that has been shown to underestimate the needs of families. Research shows that, on average, families need an income of about twice that level to cover basic expenses.[5]

We are taught that there should be some level of shame about visiting a loved one in jail. In America, we dole out tough love — especially to Black and brown bodies. While white women and families dominate welfare spaces, it is the image of the Black woman that became linked to the term "welfare queen" — thus justifying the confederacy of death that fills our political spaces to declare war on any socialised support for our poor in America. Poverty is a symptom of capitalism, an ugly and necessary by-product of the death project.

> Anti-black violence within the Americas is, of course, bound

up in a range of death-dealing activities: the subtleties of slow bloodless genocides, imprisonment, racial profiling and police brutalities, poverty, environmental racism, and community bloodshed all tally slave and post-slave death in black communities. With this, one can also track incontrovertible urbicidal practices through the razing of specific black communities, homes, buildings, and sacred sites — Africville, the African Burial Ground, the ninth ward in New Orleans, and more.[6]

Neoliberalism is what plantation politics look like now. It is the idea that you are responsible for your life in a system that is rooted in the death project, which itself is rooted in the oppression of Black and brown bodies in order for it to profit. It profits from the death and containment of our bodies, whether on Turtle Island or in Europe. Neoliberalism takes collective responsibility and makes it personal. Neoliberalism is the idea that if you can pull yourself up by your bootstraps, you'll be fine, except, of course, if you don't have any boots or have a pair without laces.

Neoliberalism is New Age politics: it's all your fault. You just didn't save enough, you didn't work hard enough, you you you… never enough.

* * *

Some people tout that your liberation is contingent upon your understanding of Hegel. I say our liberation is contingent upon our understanding of self and there is no better teacher than our ancestors. Rather than looking into the pages of books written by our conquerors, I have been seeking out the wisdom of those who have too often been silenced. In my journey, I have learned a little about the Medicine Wheel and the relationship between the mind, the body, the soul and the emotions. According to certain teachings of the Medicine Wheel, it is our individual and personal responsibility to ensure the balance between these four. I have learned about the Ghost Dance, that ceremony for the regeneration of the earth and our health. Son, imagine this world!

Our imagination, our consciousness, is the most powerful gift that we have. We invest things with power by directing our consciousness toward them. It is important that we exercise our imagination and engage it to find solutions and to envision more balanced and peaceful futures. You will often hear people telling you that it is human nature to kill, to be jealous, that the world is the way that it is because it has to be. Please son, don't ever believe this, for in doing so, your consciousness becomes locked in a very limited and powerless position.

For some, regardless of skin colour, capitalism is the golden cow. We live in a time where even some hip hop artists tell us through their lyrics that our problem is our inability to save money, buy property or get educated.

If hard work amassed wealth, people of African descent would not be poor. But this idea persists and is often touted even by many in our own communities around the world. This idea ignores the systemic exclusion that European white settler colonisation created. A recent article in the *Nation* reported that it would take African Americans two hundred and twenty-eight years to amass the wealth of a white family today.[7]

Neoliberalism speaks about personal responsibility. What about historical responsibility? Collective responsibility? Retroactive responsibility? There is no power greater than that of our ancestors. Speak their names and they will protect you.

This is not true, thankfully, for all of us. There are those who have held on to the traditions, who have kept the memories alive, who were not fooled into letting go of that which ensured not only their own spiritual survival, but those of their descendants. Practices such as Santaria, Obeah, Voodoo — misunderstood and misrepresented by the West but held as sacred in bloodlines through which Africa courses. The rebellions and revolts of enslaved Africans owe much to these belief systems, with the most famous, of course, being the Haitian Revolution, where Toussaint Louverture and Jean-Jacques Dessalines were able to do what no other had done before them: liberate themselves and their people from the barbarity of slavery. Just think, my son — Haiti, now known for its poverty and natural disasters, was the first free Black republic in the so-called New World. Imagine a nation of Blacks who rose up from the indignities of enslavement, who broke free from their shackles, a nation who based their revolt on the battle cry that ignited the French Revolution: *Liberty, Equality and Fraternity*. And what would Haiti get for its bravery, its vision, its bold ambition?

What have we been blindfolded to?

It is no coincidence that all human beings around the world have had some practice of ancestor worship. What we call worship could be looked at as respect. What greater respect can you show yourself than by knowing your ancestors?

We have not only had our sense of space/place shifted, we also have had our pasts erased. And what has happened to our land?

My nephew's parents met in Brooklyn — a part of New York City that now boasts the most expensive rents and real estate in the US. It is not a coincidence that when I go there to visit, the people from my past are no longer there.

Indeed, empirical evidence shows that the death of a black sense of place and the attendant descriptors of decay, incarceration, deportation, pollution, and displacement are reminiscent, but certainly do not twin, a plantation logic that spatialized the complementary workings of modernity, land exploitation, and anti-black violence.[8]

We did not know that our existence there was meant to be temporary.

* * *

Who owns the land?

One could argue that it is no coincidence that my brother ended up in jail. It is no coincidence that he had the life he did. Many would be quick to say, "but he chose his path, so he had to deal with it." But for many of us growing up in a city that was not there to nurture us, but to destroy us, one could argue that the decisions he made were rational ones.

The documentary *13th* does an excellent job of introducing the work of Michelle Alexander, the author *The New Jim Crow*, and showing the connection between the "war on drugs" and racist policies that greatly impact poor communities. For example, although whites and Blacks use drugs at about the same rate, Blacks are more likely to spend time in jail for this nonviolent offense — often serving disproportionately longer sentences than their white counterparts.

The US's history with drugs ought to be re-examined. Surely something is amiss when a country known for its freedom imprisons more of its citizens than any other country in the world.

I know that this prison system, or what is now known as the "prison-industrial complex" is but a continuation of slavery, a way to profit from our bodies. Whether we're talking about Grenfell or Katrina; Flint, Michigan, or Saudi Arabia — Black people, despite our global accomplishments — continue to be among the least protected in the societies in which we find ourselves. Whether it's the mysterious death of Alexander Bengtsson, a Black Swedish politician, whose dead body was found in a burnt-out car to which the police responded "no foul play" (despite a history of death threats which could even be seen on his blog), the increase in hate crimes in the US and Europe, or the cyclical regurgitation of the N-word debate here in the media, anti-Black racism is alive and well all over the world. And something must be done.

* * *

The day that my nephew and I went to visit his father in the penitentiary, we took a bus from the Port Authority to Pittsburgh, Pennsylvania. It was in the middle of winter, February, and he had already been locked up since the previous summer. It was a clear, crisp, sunny winter day — typical of the days of East Coast winter months, and so unlike the dark winters of Northern Europe.

Your Uncle Gerry has my mother's maiden name, Balbirsingh. Did you know that the first documented murder in the United States in retaliation for 9/11 was a Sikh man in Texas with the very same name? Uncle Gerry's son, Gerard Jr, and I meet uptown, in Harlem on a Friday evening. He's tall and handsome. He looks a lot like you.

Before boarding the bus to Pittsburgh, my nephew and I go out to eat at Harlem Shake. We sit across from each other and he bows his head in prayer before his meal. We talk about Black liberation, aliens and history. We talk about colonisation and he, like so many other people, is surprised to learn that Christopher Columbus never set foot on US soil. Our bus drive is at night and when we arrive to Pittsburgh, it's very early in the morning. Your uncle's childhood friend, Mike, meets us at the bus stop. We eat breakfast at a local hotel. We then drive to Sharon, Pennsylvania, which is where my brother lived before he was locked up. Your uncle got locked up due to something he says the justice system calls "profiting." A suspect faces a charge with substantial time attached to it. If the suspect delivers names, however, they face a significantly shorter prison sentence. Other times charges are lodged against the suspect who is given a choice to either admit to the crime and face, as in my brother's case, four years, or go to court and risk being put away for as many as thirty years. If you're poor in the US — justice is not so blind.

When I learned through Facebook that your uncle had been imprisoned, it compounded the depression, or spiritual crisis if you will, that I had already begun to feel taking its toll — and in this energy I decided to delete my Facebook account. I had had it for several years, since the inception of Facebook, and had made connections with friends I'd had no idea I would be in touch with again in my lifetime. But that day, as I read the post that a careless person had made and which had revealed to me that my brother had been imprisoned, my world completely and utterly spiralled around me, seeming to drain to the ground, leaving me completely without energy or spirit.

So, while sitting in my mother's bedroom in Brooklyn, I got the idea to visit your uncle. I would only be in the US for a few weeks. At least that was the plan at that point, and I had just received a freelance job and calculated that not only could I take this trip to Pittsburgh to visit your uncle in jail, but that perhaps I could pay to fly in my nephew to New York from Atlanta, and that we could make this trip together from New York. I figured that it would give us some much-needed time to catch up — the last time I had seen him he was about twelve — and I had hoped that it could cultivate more of a relationship between us.

It is capitalism that gets in the way of family, yet it is interesting to see how little we put words to it. But let's pull together some empirical evidence here before we go on, before I get deeper into my story. There was once a great historian who would later go on to become the first prime minister of a "newly independent" Trinidad and Tobago, the land that our family is from. This historian's name was Dr Eric Williams, and he was a beacon in the darkness of colonial times. For hundreds of years Trinidadians of African and East Indian descent were taught that it was England that they should strive for in all that they did. Your great-grandparents, my grandparents, Hildred and Ewart Balbirsingh, were prime examples of this. As most Trinidadians and Tobagonians do, we called them "Mummy Hildred" and "Grandaddy" respectively. Curiously enough they were both raised by people other than their biological parents. This is an all-too-common occurrence in the shadow of empire.

Mummy Hildred had no shortage of pictures of Queen Elizabeth in her home; a queen whose lineage, mind you, oversaw the trans-Atlantic trade of the enslavement of our ancestors. Granddaddy cited Shakespeare and tinkered with words, very often asking us, his grandchildren, about words like "Penultimate. Do you know what that means?" However, he knew nothing about the origin of his name Balbirsingh or about the religion we are told it stems from, Sikhism. And if he did, he told us not much about it.

This is the lament of the colonial subject: we know so much about our colonial masters but know nothing about who we are. Even if we know who we are individually — who are we collectively? This is the challenge that has never gone away and is still with us: how do we become our own people in the shadow of concealment and lies?

Gerry's the quintessential older brother: He has always been protective and providing. Whenever I got in fights back in Flatbush, he'd always have my back. We shared the same friends: a motley crew of kids from the building and from the block. His friends were Caribbean rude boys and southern gentlemen who wore silk shirts and side parts that burrowed, like a road, into the bushiness of their flattops. A gold tooth was a cool thing to have, and a man was judged by the shine of his Clarks or the whiteness of his sneakers. We listened to Sister Nancy, Yellow Man and Kurtis Blow. His friends came from Guyana, Jamaica, Panama and other African diaspora nations.

When we get to Sharon, Mike takes us over to Kevin's place. Kevin is also from Brooklyn and from back in the day. He's a tall guy, and like the rest of my brother's friends, dresses in oversized hip-hop clothes. Kevin is always reppin' Brooklyn, whether it's on his t-shirt or baseball cap. While we're there, he tells us stories about my brother and him from back in the day. He tells us stories of hustling, breakdancing and parties. He tells us about how he feels the child-support system has been used to further debilitate Black men and I have to admit that it was not the first time I heard this claim. It's not that I'm against receiving some support for your child, but the mathematics, at least how I heard it, didn't really make much sense especially when you take into consideration that "Black men's average hourly wages went from being 22.2% lower than those of white men in 1979 to being 31% lower by 2015. For women, the wage gap went from 6% in 1979 to 19% in 2015."[9]

I remember Kevin from back in the day. He was always well-dressed and really intelligent, rocking IZOD shirts and Lee jeans back when I definitely couldn't afford gear like that. He's one of those people who can't help but take all the attention in the room just because he's a great storyteller. Everyone has a friend who can tell a story and a joke like Dave Chappelle. Kevin is that dude. He talked about his first and last stint in jail, how he avoided everyone by hugging his blanket around him and sitting alone on a bench. "I don't know how folks keep on getting busted, Les," he tells me. "Jail is for no one."

We soon leave to visit Gerry at jail.

As mentioned, your uncle was a really good breakdancer and New York DJ and I remember when I attended Washington Irving High School in Manhattan, getting into Mars for free. Mars was this multi-level club housed in an old warehouse in Manhattan's meatpacking district. I used to go with my two friends Ruhiya and Dorian, and our math teacher would usually tag along. Gerry played reggae on the third floor, and we had the whole building to explore for the entire night. Imagine: three fifteen-year-old girls in a nightclub, fumbling around in darkness, through maroon curtains and dancing our butts off. It was fun. It was in the late Eighties. That's when black jeans with white t-shirts and black shoes were practically a club uniform.

Gerry was also the first person to take me to the legendary Paradise Garage, still the best time I've ever had in my life. We danced until 6am: I remember doing a popular dance called "the wop" with this tall, thin, chocolate brother, like, ALL night. It was the first time I had ever partied like that but it wouldn't be the last — I was only twelve! That night we partied with the mother of his child, Shannon, who wore gold bamboo earrings, tight, stonewashed jeans and Reebok sneakers.

Gerry was also the person who taught me how to ride a bike. I learned late: I must have been eight or nine and was the only person in my building who still didn't know how. Everyone had ten speeds, banana seat or huffy bikes but I'd never had one of my own. And getting one for me wasn't high up on my parents' list either. Daddy was too busy running from his own depression and my mother was bogged down by a myriad of jobs that were needed to pay bills. Gerry was a wiz at making his own bikes. He and his friends built them from scratch and they always turned out to be the best. He taught me a lot about repairing bikes too — how to find if an inner tube had a hole in it, putting a chain on, and how to check that the axis was not bent. Riding a bike became a priceless skill that came in really handy after moving here to Denmark since it really is the best way to get around. By the time Gerry became a father he'd dropped out of school. They tried to put him in Special Education but he told them that if they did, he wasn't coming back to school. "They're kids in there who are setting the class on fire," he would say, but no one listened.

A little before this time in his life, I had already been sent to Trinidad to live with my grandparents. I'd see Gerry on the few times I visited Brooklyn. No matter how long it had been since we last saw each other, we'd ease right into our usual relationship as if we were still hanging out in front of the building on Ocean Avenue with the summer sky hanging lightly over us. Boys popped wheelies and girls popped gum. People went away to college and some got locked up. Many girls made it into adulthood and some girls raised babies — theirs, hopefully, with the help of their families.

We drive to the jail with the sound of R&B filling the silence of the car. The sun is bright and I enjoy it as we have no such brightness in Denmark at this time of year. Then we pull up to a squat building tucked behind the highways. There's wiring on top and a security tower. It hurts my stomach to think that my brother is in there. We park the car and as we walk up the pathway to the building I can't help but notice that the path is lined with little US flags.

My country, 'tis of thee,
Sweet land of liberty,
Of thee I sing;
Land where my fathers died,
Land of the pilgrims' pride,
From ev'ry mountainside
Let freedom ring!

There are two young white girls who, because of their presence here, were just as good as Black; and there were no Black people on the staff. I know that there are white folks in jail and that there are Black people who work in prisons, but I cannot help but take in this sobering sight.

James Forman Jr's *Locking Up Our Own* goes into the uncomfortable reality of how complicit our own have been in this system. He writes, "Far from ignoring the issues of crime by blacks against other blacks, African-Americans officials and their constituents have been consumed by it."[10] This issue, as we can see, is clearly not one of black and white — but, as discussed above, Michelle Alexander's work makes a strong point in connecting our modern penal system to that of slavery, which becomes even stronger when we take into account the role that prison labour plays in the American economy.

The prison guards do not line you up until the actual visiting hour starts. This means that the prisoners are all sitting at their windows, waiting for their visitors to arrive. When visiting hour starts, we must go through the security check. When we get there I see my brother in his orange jumpsuit sitting at this window and a whole line of others, dressed the same way. When we all are allowed in I can't help but notice that there is one prisoner who just sits there: his visitor never made it.

When I had told someone that I was going to visit my brother they said, "When you get there, you'll see people who really don't know how to behave. It's sad." I felt compelled to tell this person about the generational legacy of imprisonment, how for many Americans, jail has always been something they have had to contend with in one way or another. For too many, jail is more American than apple pie. The issue for me is that the US must reform its prison systems.

The first thing my brother tells me when I pick up the

telephone is, "Hey Lesley, do you know how much money you can make teaching in South Korea?"

I laugh.

Now that your uncle is out he seems to be all about the business. Many years ago, before his last lock-up, I remember how frustrated he was becoming before securing his last job. He was looking for a job, but was experiencing difficulty, due to his previous convictions. I remember my brother telling me how he couldn't understand why if he did a crime and did the time — which, let's face it, after Clinton's draconian drug laws of 1994 that ensured the lock-up rate for nonviolent crimes went astronomically high — how come he couldn't just live? How come he couldn't vote?

Whenever my brother is searching for a job, he always calls me to, as he puts it, "Hook my resume up for me." This time however, he has to stay in a halfway house and every time I speak to him there is a new development, the last one being that fortunately, he has been given the job back that he held before his imprisonment.

Right before my brother got his last job he had lost a job he really liked because of his record. "How am I supposed to pay my bills and stay out of trouble when nobody gives me a chance? It's like I feel like I don't have a choice. It's not like I killed somebody or that I'm even in contact with the patients in the building. And it's preparing food — I could do that. I like that. I had a car — I was going to get me a Cadillac CTS, but I couldn't get that so I got a Nissan Altima instead…"

"I don't know what you're talking about," I tell him, "I don't know anything about cars." At thirty-five years old, I still don't have my license.

"I'm stressed now." He lets out a sigh. "What you doing now, anyway?"

"Chillin'."

"Chillin'," he repeats, saying after me. "Damn Les, you gotta say that shit with more soul. What they doing to your soul up there in Denmark?" We laugh. He continues, "I was reading up on Denmark the other day. You guys are like ten years behind on shit." We laugh again. "How they expect someone to get their life together? And that shit that turned up, that was more than seven years ago…"

My brother had done a couple of stints in jail — he's had even more brushes with the law.

"I need a job man. A j-o-b," he begins again. "Man, all you need to do is get a job, work there, get benefits. All I really need is to pay my rent and my car note. I don't need any more than that. I ain't trying to be no gangster…"

My sister, brother and I survived a turbulent childhood. We survived it and in a lot of ways, my sister and my brother represent different paths. Your Aunt Shelley went on to find love, lose this love through death and build her life up again. She has become a source of great support and integrity in my life. When I see my brother and our old friends from Brooklyn together, I experience the opportunity to be completely myself in a way that only sharing a common past could create.

I'm not a sociologist, I'm just a sister whose brother is not only experiencing some of the consequences of past decisions, but at the same time merely looking for a break. He is fifty years old and has two kids and has just been released from a four-year stint in prison.

What are the prospects for my brother? How will he get himself out of this? How can I help him?

The last time I spoke to your uncle he had just received the news that he was being released from the halfway house he was required to stay in for six months. Luckily for him, he's getting out early.

Years ago on that telephone call with him he said, "That's why I tell my son he needs to go to school. He needs to get himself a vocation. He needs to get a job." He continues now about his son. "He need to get out of that rap game and get himself a skill. It's all about a job." And I think about the way my brother spins Yellowman, Buju Banton and how his son is now married, holding it down and is, by all standards, a success.

I think about how your face lit up like a sun-drenched beach whenever you were around my brother the last time you saw him. I remember how my brother, your uncle, used to think he was Jamaican and how one day he took me to Campus Quarters with him and how he put my initials "lab" in for the high score (Centipede, I think was the game) and how we discovered together what it had spelled. I remember how one of my classmates had told me on my way home from P.S. 152 that my brother had killed a boy and how one day I saw him and my mother, dressed in black, go off to a funeral. I remember his words, the same even to this day, "He said he could swim. I think he caught a cramp. He was in too deep. I ran out to help and the next thing I know they was doing resuscitation on him and the ambulance was there…" And I wonder what it must feel like seeing someone die in front of you, someone you want very much to live, but no matter how much you will it, it does not happen. My brother was about fourteen years old.

"Awright Les." He exhales, "I gotta go. Imma go take a shower, go to the store…"

Whenever I travel to New York, my brother is always there. He loves to hit the road, driving between states, showing up on us, surprising us. When I come to New York, he takes me to Nostrand Avenue, where we get roti, doubles, and phoulori. However, this trip my brother is not able to do that, so this time, I visit him.

And I am again filled with hope. I hope that there are people out there who will see the beautiful human being that my brother is and give him a chance. I hope that they will be able to do what my brother, then only a child, could not do for his friend on that day.

But my brother, like all of us, always creates ways out of paths where there seem to be none. I know he will rise up and be about something. But what about the countless others who are left in this system? Whose human rights are being trampled upon every day because they were convicted of a crime? We are inventive people; we must create paths where there are none.

In the most recent conversation I had with your uncle, he told me he was going on a date. I'm sure he's going to be more than okay.

Radical Healing Plants

Dear Son,

Your father is right about many things, but there was one thing about which he was very wrong. When we were a young family, he'd say sometimes how much he admired me because although I had a challenging background, I hadn't let it keep me back in life.

What I have learned since then is that many of us, many people who have suffered early childhood trauma — in my case being shuffled about, attacked in school, beaten by my own father (to name a few) — often seem to get through life pretty well, and are even often over-achievers like myself, until they reach their thirties and forties. This is when the demons start to claw their way past your veil of consciousness, spiking your nerves, your adrenaline, threatening even your sanity.

I was lucky. Others, not so much — these are usually the people who end up homeless. Being in Denmark has allowed me the space to break down and to build myself up again. To slash and burn like our ancestors of the past. I had your father and your grandmother who were able to take care of you on the days I felt as though I couldn't get out of bed. I was able to open my business after I quit my job teaching at the school so that I could stay home and work in order to earn money and take the time I needed to heal. I am blessed with an amazing doctor through the Danish healthcare system who cares about me and listens to me with a patience and tenderness that I know is not just reserved for me, but for all of her patients. I had access to a decent unemployment insurance for the short period of time I was unable to join the work market. In this time I was able to get back to breath, reassess my life and rebuild it on an even stronger and more authentic foundation. I sought refuge in nature, calypso, cassava and okra.

God bless the Black woman who mothers here in Denmark.

It is a different Denmark to the one I first arrived in eighteen years ago. I've been teaching corporate and financial English to corporations here in Denmark and I do enjoy meeting Denmark this way. Most of my students have been amazing and I am truly grateful for the many opportunities that I have had and continue to receive here in Denmark.

For the past few weeks, every evening, I hear helicopters hovering in the usually uncluttered skies of Copenhagen, a sound that takes me back to New York. There's been gang violence and random shootings, with a Nigerian man shot seven times by an unknown and still un-apprehended perpetrator, and quite recently a young boy, sixteen years old, shot six times, to death.

Yesterday I went for a walk with one of my former students, Diab. I first met Diab at the school in which I used to teach when he was just in the fourth grade. He would later be in the class I would take over when I started to work there full-time. It has been such a gift to see him grow and navigate life here in Denmark. Ever since he was young he has had a serious expression on his face — slow to smile but once you get to know him he warms up. Every so often, we meet to catch up and walk though Copenhagen together, he filling me in on his life. Because of the neighbourhood in which he was raised and still lives, and because he is Palestinian, he has grown up having been stopped and searched by the police, although he has never been caught in any criminal act. This is the reality for many young men here.

Despite this he thrives. During our walk yesterday he told me about his recent trip to Turkey where he travelled with his little brother, Belal. I know his family as I've been invited on a few occasions to eat with them and I've even met his extended family on the day that he graduated from high school. He told me how welcomed he felt in Turkey, how there to be a Palestinian is to be met with warmth, and even how once he and his brother were eating in a restaurant when the manager, upon hearing there was a Palestinian in his restaurant, came out to greet him with a hug. There are so many around the world who have been uprooted from home, who must deal with this trauma and still shine. He does this so well and I am so proud to be privy to his story.

While we walked through the centre of Copenhagen I bumped into several former students, all of whom met me with hugs and warm greetings. My eighteen years here have been fruitful. "You're famous," he jokes and tells me of his recent decision to study in Copenhagen so that he can be there for his little brother.

A few months ago, the international news picked up the tragic story of the murder of the Swedish journalist Kim Wall. Her death has had many in Denmark reeling with anguish. A meeting was called by a group of other female activists, and together we tried to figure out a way forward in a country that is very reluctant to admit that despite its reputation for gender equality, there still exists a toxic masculinity — did you know that since the beginning of this year, *two women a month* have been murdered by intimate partners?

Last January when a group of us organised the Women's March here in Copenhagen, the press kept on asking me, "But why in Denmark? There is no gender inequality here!" It is true that when compared to many other countries, there is more gender equality here. But just because it's better than other countries, doesn't mean that there is no room for improvement. There is still the gender pay gap, multiple cuts to assistance for women fleeing from the violence of their partners, harassment of women in real life and on the internet. Yes, it is much safer than other countries, but there are still issues that must be addressed.

Violence against women is a global affair.

There were many times when my family feared for our lives in the wake of my father's anger. Perhaps this is why this issue is so close to me and I will always be committed to ensuring that there is awareness around this. For as long as I live I will always think about the children and the women who are often caught in a system with very little support to be had, even in a country as progressive as Denmark sees itself to be.

Very often I hear from my students, "You always ask me questions that make me think!" In a way, that's all I want to do, through my writing, is to get people to think.

I am not writing this to disrespect the country in which I have given birth to you and chosen to raise you. I am writing this to you because I am invested in making this an even better country, as long as I am here. All my life I've always had this nagging vision that the world could be a better place, and I will never give up this dream.

* * *

Word has it that *ayahuasca* is all the rage in Brooklyn. Funny that. I'm not sure this is a bad thing though. The first time I came across ayahuasca was a few years ago, and it was in connection with treating trauma and addiction. What I had read intrigued me, and I knew it was something I was open to trying in my own journey to healing. Throughout the years, since I consciously began this journey of radical healing (which has been filled with many successes and some not so much), I have found silence and meditation helpful. I have consulted alternative healers and paid more attention to spirit. I have worked through what knowledge of my ancestors I have, and sought out information about all the cultures that I come from. This has been fortifying and I will continue with these practices.

A few months ago, one of my oldest Danish friends called me up. "You want to come to an ayahuasca retreat with me?" I had the opportunity to meet Mother Aya, as many initiates of this ritual lovingly refer to the energy you may meet when in the presence of her, and I took it. After allowing her into my life, I must say, I do not think it is a bad thing that she has come to the West. We are sick and we need healing.

Together with about twenty-seven other, mostly Danish, people I spent two nights in a large room full of mattresses and buckets out in the Danish countryside. For two nights, we worked with a shaman who played *icacaros* and I was taken on a journey that, once completed, had managed to reset me. One of the things Mother Aya is known to do is put you in touch with gratitude. The first night I cried for hours as I thought about your grandmother, your father's mother, someone who I haven't spent so much time with since the separation of your father and me. All I wanted to do was to run to her and rub her feet, tell her how thankful I am for her and all that she has done.

Mother Aya made me think about your father and how, together, we created you. I was reminded of the love that was necessary to spark your life, and I cried in gratitude of the presence your father has had in your life. I cried as I thought about your name, and how fitting it was that your name is the Hawaiian word for the ocean, that place full of history, that place full of memory. I left this retreat fully renewed, with a closer affinity to the interconnectedness of it all, and especially grateful to the other participants. It was an intense weekend, where we all showed up not just for personal healing, but for collective healing as well. I couldn't help but think how much the world needs this. One of the people that I was reminded of during my ayahuasca journey was my childhood friend India, and I was reminded of how much I missed her and the emptiness I had in my heart due to this.

And then a funny thing happened the other day. Throughout the years I have tried to find her and her mother Willie-Mae. I've searched for India many times on Facebook — but one weekend, after a period of intense meditation in a Medicine Wheel I had constructed on Anholt, something urged me to search again. And I found her.

Nothing can quite capture the joy I felt in finding her. I learned that she now lived in Georgia and her mother, sadly, had passed years ago from leukaemia. When I spoke to her I was reminded of that laughter she and her mother possessed, that smile that pushed through even in the most challenging of times. India and her mother have always been hard workers, believers in the redemptive properties of working towards goals in such a way that I often wonder why it is that we speak about the Protestant work ethic, but not that of the Africans and those of her diaspora?

Lately, I've been particularly enamoured with Édouard Glissant's *Caribbean Discourse*. I read it slowly, savouring his words. He writes:

> There is a difference between the transplanting (by exile or dispersion) of a people who continue to survive elsewhere and the transfer (by the slave trade) of a population to another place where they change into something different, into a new set of possibilities.

There are the forced migrations that the European

enslavement of Africans instigated, which Africa and her descendants are still recovering from, and there are other forced migrations. The migrations of African Americans up north from the south, running from white terror. I think about Willie-Mae and her beginnings in Sumter, South Carolina. The migrations of African Americans to the Caribbean, in search of freedom. The migrations of people of African descent back to Africa — in search of a dignity and life that has never been allowed in European colonies. The migrations of people from Iran due to brutal regimes and meddling US interventionist policies. The migrations from the many countries in Africa due to foreign-financed wars such as Eritrea and Congo. The migrations of Palestinians due to the land theft. The migrations of those from Iraq, Syria and Afghanistan fleeing war. There are the forced migrations due to natural disasters coupled with an unsympathetic state, as we saw with Katrina, which displaced tens of thousands, many still living in exile. Or those of Grenfell Tower in London.

Your grandparents migrated to the US in search of a better life. Their migration was encouraged, if not just to offset any success that African Americans may have been experiencing. I have migrated to Europe, in search of relief from the misnomer of the New World — in this system, words are devoid of any real meaning; often they represent the exact opposite of what they appear.

I have moved so much in my life. As a child, it was back and forth to Trinidad, away from my parents and then with them. In Brooklyn, we would have to move quite often due to my father's music, or due to my parent's inability to pay rent. I left home when I was sixteen and the number of times I have moved since then is uncountable. I have lived in every neighbourhood in Copenhagen in the eighteen years that I've been here. All of this moving makes it difficult to have roots, to stay in touch.

Throughout the years, before the advent of social media, I often wondered about the children I had gone to school with in Brooklyn, in Trinidad. With Facebook came the opportunity to reconnect. I have reconnected with high-school friends from New York and Trinidad. And throughout the years I have tried to find India and Willie-Mae.

Willie-Mae and India were the only stability I had as a child, growing up. Speaking to India reminded me of their forever-open front door. I'd often go with them to visit their family at the projects in Coney Island. I was introduced to African American cuisine through them: collard greens and smoked neck bones, grits. India and I would often walk to Newkirk Avenue to buy eggrolls from the Chinese restaurant and she introduced me to spiced ham, which she'd buy by the slice at the local deli. On summer days, we'd jump double-dutch in front of the building with the other girls who lived there, Nikki, Sandy and Andrea from up the block. We'd do each other's hair, whether it was cornrows or using hot combs to straighten our curls out. We'd rub cocoa butter into our skin and Vaseline our baby hair. We popped bubble gum and witnessed the birth of hip hop.

We saw local girls, teenagers, get pregnant and boys get locked up. We saw a reality dawning upon us that made me feel as though I was losing control. I'd go to church with Willie-Mae and India — I loved the liveliness of the Black church as opposed to what I thought to be my mother's boring Catholic service.

Willie-Mae also loved Trinidad. She loved the food and the people and the culture. She was so beautiful to me and I had always thought of her as one of my mothers. When I was sent to live in Trinidad she'd write me letters. Willie-Mae spoke with such an authentic Trinidadian accent she even fooled Granddaddy, whom she had convinced she was from Laventille. He died believing she was Trinidadian.

Son, we have always had a global presence, making worthwhile contributions to any culture we have found ourselves in. There have been struggles, as can be seen in these tales I hand down to you, and there have been successes. This is what I can give you — hold on to it, keep it close and never believe otherwise. We are inventive people, son, paving ways where there otherwise seem to be none.

May the ancestors continue to protect you and guide you.

Àse, as the Yoruba say, *and so it will be*.

Conclusion

As mentioned in these letters, much of what I share with you did not come to me until I was between the ages of thirty and forty. When I was faced with such deep and personal crises, it led me to examine the ideas in the West that we have of mental disease, early childhood trauma and even how this is related to the social structures in which we have been born.

Up until this reckoning with myself, I had thought that I had beaten the system. I was successful by many other people's standards: I had not only moved to another country but, by all appearances, was flourishing. I had managed to forge a career here based on my writing and teaching and was able to accumulate the material trappings that many associate with success. I knew something was wrong, however, when I moved into my newly bought apartment and cried throughout unpacking boxes and boxes of my life thus far in Denmark.

This propelled me to search for answers. While therapy is a must, it is not always financially accessible and, besides, living in such a racially homogenous society as Denmark brought into relief for me how important it was for me to understand who I was and from whence I came. Although this desire has always been with me my entire life (one could say that I was born this way) it was not until this time in my life that memory came flooding back to me, seeming to threaten my very existence.

I am thankful for this breakdown. A wise person once said that you cannot have a breakthrough until you have a breakdown — and I full-heartedly agree with this. I knew that part of my task was to rid myself of the social vanity and fear of failing so that I could start anew, fresh — slash and burn. Having to open my heart to humility brought me closer not only to my own personal power, but to the power of my ancestors, whom I have felt with me especially when I speak their names, and who revealed who were my true friends.

While not everyone would choose to handle this situation in the way that I did, I am forever thankful for the path I chose as I recognised how universal this was, this growing older, this growing inability to carry on as if nothing was the matter.

I have found the process of getting older quite unlike most accounts given by the media and popular culture. While we are encouraged to think about aging as a disability, I have found through experience that there is a wisdom, a liberation to be had by this process. I was lucky, however, that because of the very social systems in place in Denmark and the support of my ex-husband I did not end up on the street. The reality is that if I had been in the States, this story could have gone another way. Not everyone is this lucky and this has only strengthened my conviction that having a home should never, ever, come down to luck. It is a universal right. As major metropolitan cities such as New York, London and even Copenhagen have invested much in development and gentrification, one must ask: where do the less financially able people go? While in the US the answer seems to be prison, what is the answer here in Europe? As more and more buildings go up in Copenhagen, less and less affordable housing can be found. How can this be addressed?

One of the integral foundations of the West is the ego. We are an extremely individualistic society — and throughout the years, Denmark has been making strides in catching up with the rest of the West in this. Social welfare, it could be argued, only works when in a racially homogenous society; but I would like to challenge this idea and advocate for the importance of ensuring that the weakest in society are included. A country's greatest resource is not its wealth but its people — and I do hope that we are entering an age where this is enacted not only in our policy but in practice as well.

Notes

Introduction

1   Steve Russell, "Did the Deaths of 50 Million Indians Cause Climate Change?," *Indian Country Today* (online), 13 March 2015.

2   In *Expat: Women's True Tales of Life Abroad*, edited by Christina Henry De Tessan, Seal Press, 2002.

In the Beginning

1   Daniel Quinn, *The Story of B*, Bantam Books, 1997, p. 252.

2   Ben Pako, "This High-Ranking Viking Warrior was a Woman," *Smithsonian Magazine* (Online), 11 September, 2017.

3   Saxo Grammaticus, *Saxo Grammaticus: History of the Danes*, translated by Peter Fisher, BOYE6, 1979, p. 212.

4   Noel Malcolm, "There were hundreds of Africans in Tudor England, and none of them were slaves: *Black Tudors*, Miranda Kaufmann review," *Telegraph* (online), 21 October 2017.

Stories are Life

1   Emil Eggert Scherrebeck, "Har du også glemt, hvorfor det hedder kolonialvarer?", *Information* (online), 3 January, 2015.

2   Jon Stone, "British people are proud of colonialism and the British Empire, poll finds," Independent (online), 19 January, 2016.

When Terrorism Has a White Face

1   Tom Turula, "The Nordic countries are the worst in the world for making friends, according to expats," *Business Insider* (online), 7 September, 2017.

2   Martin Amis, "Martin Amis, the Art of Fiction No. 151,"
     The Paris Review (online), Spring 1990
3   Mette Wiggen, "Scandinavia: the radical right meets the
     mainstream," *The Conversation* (online), 4 September,
     2017.
4   Julia Suárez-Krabbe, *Race, Rights and Rebels: Alternatives
     to Human Rights and Development from the Global South*,
     Rowman and Littlefield, 2015, p. 16
5   Ed Simon, "How 'white people' were invented by a
     playwright in 1613," *Aeon* (online), 12 September 2017.
6   "Race," *New Oxford American Dictionary*, Third Edition,
     Oxford University Press, 2010 (Online)
7   Zora Neale Hurston, *Their Eyes Were Watching God*, Vira-
     go, 1986
8   @MissTeju_Global, 15 August 2017
9   "Law of Jante," *Wikipedia* (online), last updated 10 Oc-
     tober, 2017.

What Whispers the Water?

1   Jason Hickel, "Our best shot at cooling the planet might
     be right under our feet," *Guardian* (online), 10 Septem-
     ber, 2016.

Brooklyn Is War

1   Quoted in Louise Edwards, "'Queen Mary' Folk Song:
     A Commemoration of 1878 Fireburn," *Oberlin College Li-
     brary – Omeka Projects* (online), 14 April, 2014.
2   Lorena Infante Lara, "Your Childhood Experiences Can
     Permanently Change Your DNA," *Smithsonian Magazine*
     (online), 14 September, 2017.
3   Leonard Peltier, "On Our Murdered Native Woman,"
     CounterPunch (online), 1 September 2017.

Cunt-Tree: The Map to Liberation

1   This poem is inspired by a conversation with the South

African Black-consciousness scholar, activist and artist Simmi Dullay, who spoke about her unpublished thesis "Exploring Exile as Persona and Social Transformation through Critical Reflection and Creative and Artistic Expression" (2010) and her artwork "Love in Exile" (2009).

2   "Country," *New Oxford American Dictionary*, Third Edition, Oxford University Press, 2010 (Online)

3   "Cunt," *New Oxford American Dictionary*, Third Edition, Oxford University Press, 2010 (Online)

4   "Tree," *New Oxford American Dictionary*, Third Edition, Oxford University Press, 2010 (Online)

The Forgotten Fathers

1   Mychal Denzel Smith, "What Liberals Get Wrong about Identity Politics," *New Republic* (online), 11 September, 2017.

2   Combahee River Collective, "A Black Feminist Statement," *Public Women, Public Words: A Documentary History of American Feminism, Volume 2*, edited Dawn Keeley, Rowan & Littlefield, 2005, p. 79

3   Ibid, p. 80

4   Édouard Glissant, "The Known, the Uncertain," *Caribbean Discourse: Selected Essays*, University Press of Virginia, 1989, p. 93

5   Édouard Glissant, "Cross-Cultural Poetics," *Caribbean Discourse: Selected Essays*, University Press of Virginia, 1989, p. 106

6   Ibid p. 117

7   Langston Hughes, "Harlem (What Happens to a Dream Deferred?)," *The Collected Works of Langston Hughes Volume Three: The Poems: 1951-1967*, University of Missouri Press, 2001, p. 74

8   Felix Blake, quoted in Sharon Dudley, *Music from Behind the Bridge: Steelpan Aesthetics and Politics in Trinidad and*

Tobago, Oxford University Press, 2007, p. 4

9   Sonjah Stanley Niaah, *Dancehall: From Slave Ship to Ghetto*, University of Ottowa Press, 2010, pp. 35-36

The Mothers of Memory: The Violence of Silence (A Search for Womanhood, a Search for Truth)

1   Carole Boyce-Davis, *Moving Beyond Boundaries: International Dimensions to Black Women Writing*, New York University Press, 1995 p. 31.

2   Amelia Meyer, "Role of the 'Matriarch Elephant'," *Elephants Forever* (online), 2015.

3   Brooke Axtell, "Black Women, Sexual Assault and the Art of Resistance," *Forbes* (online), 25 April, 2012.

The Birth of a Mother

1   Niels Arbøl, "Danish children get stressed in our institutions", *Jyllands Posten* (Online), 1 September, 2017

Denmark's Real National Treasures

1   BBC News, "Merkel says German multicultural society has failed", *BBC News* (online), 17 October 2010

The Lion Learns to Write: A Visit to My Brother in Jail

1   Sylvia A Harvey, "2.7 Million Kids Have Parents in Prison. They're Losing Their Right to Visit," the *Nation* (online), 2 December, 2015.

2   https://www.facebook.com/berniesanders/posts/14126 04515461215

3   Personal correspondence, 22 September, 2017

4   Katherine McKittrick, "On Plantations, Prisons, and a Black Sense of Place," *Social and Cultural Geography*, Vol. 12, No. 8, December 2011, p. 951.

5   "Child Poverty," *National Center for Children in Poverty (NCCP)* (online), 2017.

6 Katherine McKittrick, "On Plantations, Prisons, and a Black Sense of Place," *Social and Cultural Geography*, Vol. 12, No. 8, December 2011, p. 952.

7 Joshua Holland, "The Average Black Family Would Need 228 Years to Build the Wealth of a White Family Today," *Nation*, 8 August 2016.

8 Katherine McKittrick, "On Plantations, Prisons, and a Black Sense of Place," *Social and Cultural Geography*, Vol. 12, No. 8, December 2011, p. 951.

9 Molly Redden and Jana Kasperkevic, "Wage gap between white and black Americans is worse today than in 1979," *Guardian*, 20 September 2016.

10 James Forman Jr, *Locking Up Our Own*: *Crime and Punishment in Black America*, Farrar, Straus and Giroux, 2017

Conclusion

1 Édouard Glissant, "Reversion and Diversion," *Caribbean Discourse: Selected Essays*, University Press of Virginia, 1989, p. 14

Acknowledgements

Thank You

Anni Bomholtz, bushmamma@well_being_guru, the oracle@Dakini_Goddess, Angolan poet, writer & healer Aaiún Nin, Larissa Imfurayase, Eva Afewerki, Peter Stanners & the Murmur for publishing some of the pieces in this book for the first time, Amber Payne and NBCBLK for supporting my work, Marronage the journal for their vision & publishing another version of The Conquest of Kairi, Opal Palmer Adisa Ph.D for publishing another version of Cunt-Tree: the Map to Liberation in *Interviewing the Caribbean*, her daughter Teju Adisa-Farrar for her wisdom, talent and vision, Ida Marie Therkildsen & Mette Moestrup for being such bad-ass Danes, Laila Mortensen for reading and providing invaluable feedback, Angela Cruz @ Niakwa Healing Arts for being my spiritual rock, Paulette Robinson for keeping me sane through laughter, food and memories of Flatbush, Intisar Abioto for being, Feven Mekonnen Istefanos, Patrick Anthony for always looking out! Anna Riis, for being such a dedicated doctor, Christian Von Staffeldt, Puff, Jose Arce & Julia Suárez for the inspiration, Debbie Cowell for your intelligence, patience, talent and dotting my I's whenever I forget, Jens Lundvang, Shelley-Ann Balbirsingh D'Anna for being the best big sister, my nephew Gerard for being an example of integrity, my neice Geriah (we miss you), Mrs. Stein, my fourth grade teacher at P.S. 152 who imprinted me with compassion through her lessons, Ms. Pinder at Diamond Vale Elementary School who took me under her wing, my brother Gerry for keeping your head up in the hardest of situations, ancestor Brook Stephenson, and the Rhode Island Writer's Colony—thank you, to all my students past and present (go get it!), ancestor Willie Mae Walls for teaching me with so much love, to my mother for always supporting my truth and all the many other folks in Denmark, the U.S, in Trinidad and Tobago and all over the world who support my work.

Repeater Books

is dedicated to the creation of a new reality. The landscape of twenty-first-century arts and letters is faded and inert, riven by fashionable cynicism, egotistical self-reference and a nostalgia for the recent past. Repeater intends to add its voice to those movements that wish to enter history and assert control over its currents, gathering together scattered and isolated voices with those who have already called for an escape from Capitalist Realism. Our desire is to publish in every sphere and genre, combining vigorous dissent and a pragmatic willingness to succeed where messianic abstraction and quiescent co-option have stalled: abstention is not an option: we are alive and we don't agree.